BETWEEN TWO FIRES

Village School

This book was donated to

Mrs Pitman

by

Your 1996 - 1997 Class

BOOK FAIR 1996

BETWEEN TWO FIRES

BLACK SOLDIERS IN THE CIVIL WAR

BY JOYCE HANSEN

The African-American Experience
Franklin Watts
New York Chicago London Toronto Sydney

For My Brothers, Victor and Arnold

Frontis: Corporal Peter Waggall of the United States Colored Troops.

Photographs copyright ©: New York Public Library, Picture Collection: pp. 2, 16, 24, 25 top, 45, 52, 70, 81, 85, 92, 95, 100, 107, 118, 121, 139; North Wind Picture Archives, Alfred, ME: pp. 8, 14, 132, 143; The Library of Congress: pp. 19, 39, 63, 69; Courtesy of The New York Historical Society, New York City: p. 25; University of Virginia, Virginia Library: p. 31; Hagley Museum and Library, Greenville, Delaware: p. 33; National Portrait Gallery, Washington, D.C./Art Resource: p. 49; Cook Collection, The Valentine Museum, Richmond, VA: p. 56; Courtesy Chicago Historical Society: pp. 74, 78; *Social Education*: p. 104; McGraighead Collection, U.S. Military Academy, West Point: p. 126.

Quotations from *The Negro's Civil War* by James McPherson, are reprinted by permission of Pantheon Books, a division of Random House, Inc. Copyright © 1965 by James McPherson. Material on page 113 is from *A Brave Black Regiment*, available from Ayer Company Publisher, Salem, N.H.

Library of Congress Cataloging-in-Publication Data

Hansen, Joyce.
Between two fires : Black soldiers in the Civil War / by Joyce Hansen.
p.   cm — (The African-American experience)
Includes bibliographical references and index.
Summary: Documents the recruitment, training, and struggles of African-American soldiers during the Civil War and examines the campaigns in which they participated.
ISBN 0-531-11151-2
1. United States—History—Civil War, 1861–1865—Participation, Afro-American—Juvenile literature. 2. Afro-American soldiers—History—19th century—Juvenile literature. [1. United States—History—Civil War, 1861–1865—Participation, Afro-American. 2. Afro-American soldiers—History—19th century.] I. Title. II. Series
E540.N3H33   1993
973.7'415—dc20
92-37381   CIP AC

Contents

Author's Note

This is not so much a book about war, but rather another chapter in the larger history of the struggle of a people for liberty and dignity. I hope that the time will come when a person's worth is not judged by how efficiently he or she can eliminate another.

I also hope that readers will come away from this book understanding that racism ultimately weakens a nation and makes victims of us all.

Joyce Hansen

Crispus Attucks is mortally wounded in the Boston Massacre.

INTRODUCTION

It was March 5, 1770. A group of men raced down Boston's King Street, led by a forty-seven-year-old black man who made his living working on ships in the Boston harbor. They were rushing to join in a protest against the oppressive taxes and laws imposed on the American colonies by the British.

As the gathering crowd confronted the British soldiers in front of the Customs House—the despised symbol of British authority—a shot rang out and the shipworker fell to the ground. There were more shots and other protesters also fell. The shipworker was Crispus Attucks, a fugitive slave who had run away from his master in Framingham, Massachusetts, twenty years before. Attucks, of African and Native American descent, was the first casualty in the Boston Massacre, and the first hero in the struggle for American independence. Five years later, the colonists would begin a revolt against British rule.

Why was Attucks willing to take up the patriot's cause, even though he himself was not free? Perhaps because he keenly understood the pain of being controlled and owned by another. Perhaps he felt that if the British loosened their reins on the colonies, then the colonial slave trade, which was controlled by England, would end. Most likely he was truly a patriot, and supported the prevalent philosophy of the importance of freedom from oppression.

Like Crispus Attucks, other Americans of African descent also willingly fought in all of America's wars, because they embraced the nation's democratic ideals—in spite of their own position in America. African Americans have gone off to war with the hope, too, of gaining freedom and political rights for themselves and their children. When the colonists marched to war to free themselves of British oppression, people of African descent in the colonies also marched off to war, but to free themselves of *colonial* oppression.

Although the colonists did not have a clear policy about accepting black men into the military, there were times when their services were welcomed. Africans served in some colonial militias during the French and Indian Wars (1754–1763), although some people in colonies with large numbers of Africans feared that if the blacks were armed, they might stage slave insurrections. In April 1775, when fighting began between colonists and British, men of color volunteered and were enlisted in the military.

Black soldiers took part in the capture of Fort Ticonderoga on May 10, 1775, and fought at the Battle of Bunker Hill in June. Two blacks, Peter Salem and Salem Poor, distinguished themselves in that battle. There were black men and white men among the Minutemen who fought the British soldiers at Lexington and Concord.

Then—even though Africans were already serving in the Continental Army—General George Washington sent recruiting offices a letter on July 9, 1775, ordering them not to accept "any deserter from the ministerial army, nor any stroller, [N]egro, or vagabond, or person suspected of being an enemy to the liberty of America nor any under eighteen years of age." A few months later, however, Lord Dunmore, British Governor of Virginia, issued a proclamation stating that all slaves and indentured servants would be freed if they joined the British army. General Washington was upset. Some of his own valuable slaves left to join the British. He modified his order and stated that free blacks would be allowed to join the Continental Army. Most of these free men were from New England.

In Virginia, Maryland, Georgia, and the Carolinas, enslaved people outnumbered free blacks, and quite a few of those in slavery ran away to the British lines, upsetting the economy of these southern colonies. The southern patriots became alarmed and, despite General Washington's order to enlist only free blacks, Virginia and Maryland began to enlist both free black men and those in slavery.

Every colony except Georgia and South Carolina had Africans fighting in their military units. The historian John Hope Franklin tells us that "of the 300,000 soldiers who served the cause of independence, approximately 5,000 were Negroes." In contrast, it has been estimated that nearly 100,000 people from the enslaved population of the thirteen colonies joined the British.*

The colonists were victorious and the American nation was born; the African nation within America

*R.D. Eno, "The Fate of the Black Loyalist," *Historical Viewpoints*, John A. Garraty, ed., Vol. I (New York: Harper and Row, 1978).

was still enslaved. Individual black soldiers who had fought in the Continental Army, along with their families, were given their freedom, and the northern states began to move toward eradicating slavery, but the Revolution did not end slavery in America as some people had hoped it would.

The Constitution, adopted in Philadelphia in 1787, allowed slavery and the slave trade to continue. Article I, Section 9 extended the slave trade until 1808 and Article IV, Section 2 stated that fugitive slaves, even when found in a free state, had to be returned to their masters.

The end of the Revolutionary War was an exciting time for most Americans. They were free of the old world of kings and nobles and could create a new society where all people were equal. Yet, for the approximately 760,000 people of African descent (700,000 slave and 60,000 semifree), equality and liberty were far in the future. They would have to fight in another terrible and bloody war before American slavery would finally end.

BLACK POPULATION, CENSUS OF 1790		
STATE	SLAVES	FREE
Maine		536
New Hampshire	157	630
Vermont		269
Massachusetts		5,369
Rhode Island	958	3,484
Connecticut	2,648	2,771
New York	21,193	4,682
New Jersey	11,423	2,762
Pennsylvania	3,707	6,531
Delaware	8,887	3,899
Maryland	103,036	8,043
Virginia	292,627	12,866
North Carolina	100,783	5,041
South Carolina	107,094	1,801
Georgia	29,264	398
Kentucky	12,430	114
Tennessee	3,417	361

Source: John Hope Franklin and Franklin Moss, From Slavery to Freedom, 6th ed. (New York: Alfred A. Knopf, 1988), 80.

I

SAVE THE UNION

Where is the American liberty? ... In its far-reaching and broad sweep, slavery has stricken down the freedom of us all ...

JOHN MERCER LANGSTON,
1855

It seemed as if the entire nation was holding its breath. After nearly two hundred years of union, the states that made up the American republic were on the verge of war with one another. The decades-old power struggle between pro-slavery and antislavery forces had come to a head over the extension of slavery into newly acquired territory, and neither side was willing to compromise. When Abraham Lincoln won the presidential election of 1860, pro-slavery activists felt that the only recourse for the South, whose economy depended on African slave labor, was to go its own way.

On December 20, 1860, South Carolina seceded from the Union. By the beginning of 1861 other Southern states had voted for secession: Alabama, Florida, Georgia, Louisiana, Mississippi, and Texas. Four more states, Virginia, North Carolina, Arkansas, and Tennessee, left the Union when the war between the states began.

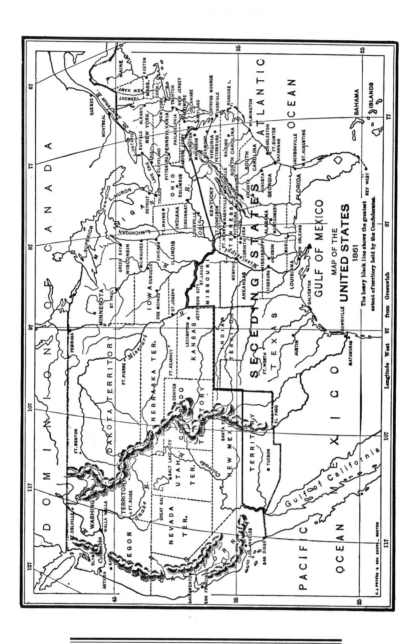

A house divided: the North and the South in 1861

What had been one nation was torn apart. There were now two presidents, capitals, congresses, flags, and sets of laws. Jefferson Davis was inaugurated President of the Confederate States of America on February 18, 1861 and began to form a presidential cabinet in Montgomery, Alabama, the first Confederate capital. At the same time, President-elect Abraham Lincoln prepared for his inauguration on March 4, 1861.

Both men said that they did not want armed conflict. However, houses rarely can be divided smoothly and amicably. The Confederates believed that they had a right to continue their way of life based on a slave economy. "Governments rest on the consent of the governed," Davis declared at his inauguration. But Abraham Lincoln asserted that "The Union of these states is perpetual, a marriage bond that cannot be broken." He was willing to compromise on slavery—he would not oppose it where it already existed. However, he would not compromise when it came to the Union. The Union could not be dissolved. No state or states had the power to defy federal authority. "In *your* hands, my dissatisfied fellow countrymen, and not in *mine*, is the momentous issue of civil war," Lincoln told the secessionist states.

Tense days followed Lincoln's inauguration. Americans on both sides watched and waited. Some prominent white abolitionists (supporters of a movement to abolish, or end, the practice of slavery), including William Lloyd Garrison, favored disunion— that is, allowing the Southerners to leave the union. They didn't think the federal government should stop the Southerners from forming their own nation. They believed that slavery would die a natural death once the secessionists went their own way.

Other abolitionists, notably Frederick Douglass,

held a different view. Douglass, one of the great leaders of the abolitionist movement, had escaped slavery and fled north from Maryland in 1837. He was an orator, a lecturer for the Massachusetts Antislavery Society, a writer and a newspaper publisher. Douglass spoke for the voiceless mass of people of African descent in America, those who were free as well as those in slavery.

Frederick Douglass agreed with the president's stand against dissolving the Union. He held that the Southerners should not be allowed to leave the federal government, taking their slaves with them. To permit this would be tantamount to abandoning the people in bondage. Douglass was incensed by the compromise Lincoln offered the Southerners—a promise not to tamper with existing slavery if the rebellion was ended.

As Douglass watched events and listened to the leaders of both sides, he became convinced that there was no place for people of color in America. Finally, the man who had had such great faith, who had believed there would be a place for men and women

Frederick Douglass, born into slavery in 1817, became an active abolitionist and an eloquent writer and orator.

of African descent in the home of the free and the brave, gave up hope.

For decades before the secession of the Southern states, abolitionists and other reformers had struggled to expose the brutal and immoral nature of slavery. Brave women and men had worked to create the Underground Railroad, a network of "safe houses" to help fugitives escaping to the North. But events continued to demonstrate that in spite of all efforts, the evils of slavery and racism were to continue.

- Fugitive slave laws forced escapees to the North to be returned to bondage in the South. One widely reported case in 1854 involved Anthony Burns, a fugitive who had escaped to Boston. Two thousand soldiers escorted Burns through the streets of Boston to a ship that carried him back to bondage in the South.
- The 1857 Dred Scott decision was a bitter disappointment to abolitionists and to men and women in slavery. Dred Scott was a black man held in slavery by an army surgeon who took him to live in Illinois, a free state, and later in Wisconsin, territory where slavery was banned. Scott sued for freedom for himself and his family and the case went all the way to the United States Supreme Court. The Court's decision stated that Scott was not a citizen under the Constitution and that residence in a free state or territory did not automatically make a person free.
- John Brown, a white abolitionist, and a small group made up of five black and thirteen white followers, raided an arsenal at Harpers Ferry, Virginia, in hopes of sparking a slave rebellion. Brown was convicted of treason, conspiracy, and murder, and was executed.

It seemed to Douglass, in the spring of 1861, that it was useless for black people to remain in America, hoping for an improvement in their status. He therefore decided to travel to Haiti to see if that would be a good country for American blacks. In the days leading up to April 13, 1861, Douglass prepared for his trip, while still watching events in America.

Everyone continued to watch and wait. Few people wanted war. However, the Confederate states wanted to control their own ports and military arsenals and forts. Jefferson Davis tried to negotiate with President Lincoln and the Republicans to take over Fort Sumter, but Lincoln's cabinet decided that the fort should remain under federal control.

On April 11, Major Anderson, federal commander of the garrison at Fort Sumter, received a message from the "Government of the Confederate States of America" demanding that he evacuate Fort Sumter. The Confederates waited for an answer. If Anderson left, they said, bloodshed would be avoided. Anderson refused.

On April 12, the Confederacy again contacted Major Anderson, asking when he would evacuate the fort. The major replied that if he received no supplies and reinforcements from the federal government by 12:00 P.M. on April 15, then he would leave Sumter.

The Confederates were not going to wait for Anderson to receive help from the federals. They informed him that the fort would be attacked in one hour. At 4:30 A.M. on April 12, 1861, Fort Sumter was bombarded by the Confederacy. On April 13, Major Anderson and his troops surrendered the fort to the Confederacy and the bloodiest war in U.S. history began. The watching and waiting had ended.

Frederick Douglass was elated. At last Lincoln had decided to fight the rebels. Douglass cancelled his trip to Haiti. He anticipated a momentous time, when the status of men and women of color in America could undergo revolutionary changes.

Lincoln called for 75,000 volunteers to put down the revolt in South Carolina and patriotism swept the North as men flocked to the recruiting stations to join the Union Army and force the rebellious Southerners back into the Union. Free northern

Fort Sumter is bombed and the
American Civil War begins.

blacks were among those who responded to the president's call. What better way could they find to show their loyalty to the federal government? This could be a chance for them to strike a blow against slavery and possibly attain full citizenship for themselves and for other blacks in bondage. If they fought for the Union, then perhaps they would be respected, as Americans, and not be restricted, as blacks, to the periphery of American life.

Jacob Dodson, a free black resident of Washington, D.C., was so encouraged and excited by the events that he wrote a letter to the secretary of war a few days after the attack on Fort Sumter. "Sir: I desire to inform you that I know of some three hundred of reliable colored free citizens of this City, who desire to enter the service for the defence of the City."[1]

Dodson must have been surprised and disappointed by the secretary's reply: "This Department has no intention at present to call into the service of the Government any colored soldiers."[2]

Black men in other Northern cities also received cold responses when they tried to form military organizations. A group of black men in Cincinnati, Ohio, held a meeting at a schoolhouse shortly after the attack on Fort Sumter. They wanted to organize a company of "Home Guards" to help defend the city. The police arrived and demanded the keys to the schoolhouse. The group was warned that a mob of whites would attack if they didn't leave.

The men then selected another building as a recruiting station to attract other blacks who might want to join the Army. The owner of the building was ordered by the police to take down the American flag that waved over his door. "We want you . . . niggers to keep out of this; this is a white man's war," the Cincinnati police told the men.[3] In Pittsburgh and Cleveland, New York City and Massachusetts, the response was the same when black men tried to form militia companies or enlist in the Army. They were flatly rejected.

Black organizations in Massachusetts petitioned the state to allow their men to join the Army and one group organized a drill company. Their petition was ignored. An organization of black men in New York City also attempted to form a drill company. The police told them they would have to stop, otherwise they could not be protected from white mob attacks.

Frederick Douglass raised his voice in frustration: "Why does the Government reject the [N]egro? Is he not a man? Can he not wield a sword, fire a gun, march and countermarch, and obey orders like any other?"[4] Douglass may have been envisioning his own sons as proud soldiers, bravely fighting against those who would make them slaves.

Even though men of African descent had fought in the American Revolution and the War of 1812, they were not allowed to serve in state militias or the regular United States Army, and their services were clearly rejected at the start of the Civil War.

One of the excuses offered in defense of slavery was that Africans were an inferior race of people. Accepting these men into the Army would destroy the stereotypical myths about men and women of color that many Americans wanted to believe. Those who were against arming black men said either that they were too cowardly to fight, or that they were too savage to be controlled in battle.

Some people expressed fear that black soldiers would enrage Southerners to the point where even the slaveholding border states still loyal to the Union (Delaware, Kentucky, Maryland, and Missouri) and certain loyal regions in the South would be lost to the Confederates. There was also fear that white soldiers would refuse to serve with black soldiers.

Abraham Lincoln declared that the war was not a war against slavery, but a war to save the Union. While the president believed that slavery was morally wrong, he was not an abolitionist. In a speech at Charleston, South Carolina, he asserted, "I am not, nor ever have been, in favor of bringing about in any way the social and political equality of the white and black races."[5]

The president understood his people. He knew that he could get Northern support to keep the Union together and stop the Southerners from seceding. However, Northerners would not go to war to free Africans from bondage. Northerners, for the most part, felt that slavery was a Southern problem, and a large number wished the problem would go away. They were tired of the abolitionists, who were viewed as trouble-making radicals, and they felt that the national crisis was caused in part by the presence of blacks and their abolitionist friends.

There were Americans, though, who had opposed slavery from the time the importation of Africans had become a large part of the American economic system. The Quakers freed their slaves in the eighteenth century, preaching that slavery was a sinful practice, especially for Christians. By the 1830s the abolitionists had begun their crusade for the removal of slavery from American life. Even before the Quakers and the abolitionists took action, Africans in America had begun to push unrelentingly for the abolishment of slavery.

As early as 1777, a group of Africans petitioned the state of Massachusetts to free "A Great Number of Blackes detained in a State of slavery."[6] By 1815 the antislavery movement in the North was growing, and free Northern men and women of color started to create organizations devoted to the abolition of slavery. One of the earliest organizations was the General Coloured Association, formed in Massachusetts around 1826. Others were the African Abolition Freehold Society, the African Female Anti-Slavery Society, and the New York Committee of Vigilance founded by David Ruggles, who was also instrumental in building the Underground Railroad.

In the 1830s, fifty separate black antislavery societies existed, most in large black communities. Black leaders emerged, in spite of laws that severely restricted the lives of free people of color. Some were:

- Frederick Douglass, fugitive from slavery, orator, and newspaper publisher.
- Henry Highland Garnet, son of an escaped slave, who was educated at the Africa Free School in New York City and became a Presbyterian minister.
- Martin Delany, freeborn, became a physician, explorer, writer and scientist. He devoted much of his life to working for the abolition of slavery. In the 1850s he was a prominent emigrationist, encouraging blacks to leave the United States. He was the first black to be commissioned a major in the Union Army.
- William Wells Brown, escaped slave, became a physician and writer. He helped many people flee to Canada. He became an army recruiting agent once men of African descent were able to enlist.
- John Mercer Langston, an antislavery lecturer and one of the first blacks elected to public office in the United States, was a United States congressman from Virginia.
- Harriet Tubman, fugitive from slavery, returned to the South many times to help others escape. She served as a spy and a nurse for the Union Army but was denied an army pension as a woman. She finally received a pension based upon her second husband's military service.
- Sojourner Truth was an orator who traveled through the country speaking against slavery.
- Frances E. Harper, freeborn in Baltimore, Maryland, became a teacher, writer, and antislavery lecturer.

FREEDOM'S JOURNAL.

"RIGHTEOUSNESS EXALTETH A NATION."

BY JNO. B. RUSSWURM.   NEW-YORK, FRIDAY, MARCH 14, 1828.   VOL. I.—NO. I

THE COLORED AMERICAN.

SAMUEL E. CORNISH,
Editor.   *New-York, Saturday, May 13, 1837.*   PHILIP A. BELL,
Proprietor.

Freedom's Journal, the first black newspaper published
in the United States, linked the free black colonies of
the North. Samuel Cornish (left) was the editor,
and John Russworm (right) was co-editor.

(*Top left*) Major Martin Delaney was the first black soldier
commissioned as a field officer in the Union army. (*Top right*)
Harriet Tubman, born about 1820 in Maryland, acted
as nurse, scout, and intelligence agent for the Union armies.
(*Above*) Sojourner Truth, born in upstate New York around
1797 and freed in 1827, was a powerful voice against slavery.

These voices, raised against slavery before and during the war, ultimately influenced the government.

By the late 1800s, most Northern states had passed laws abolishing slavery. However, that did not mean that black people in the North could fully participate in American life.

Isaac J. Hill, who became a Union soldier, was born and raised in Philadelphia. He wrote in his *Sketch of the Twenty-ninth Regiment of Connecticut Colored Troops*, "I was brought up with a limited education, not being permitted to go to school, for it was against the laws of the state for a white person to teach a colored child."[7]

With few exceptions, blacks could not attend school with whites, own property or businesses, hold certain jobs, or vote. In New York City, black men had to own property worth at least $250 in order to vote. White males were not subject to this requirement. Free blacks in Maryland had to have a license in order to sell tobacco, wheat, or corn. Finding steady employment was always a problem, even for those blacks who were artisans and craftsmen.

Abraham Lincoln went to war because he wanted the United States to remain one nation. The Confederate states went to war because they wanted to determine their own way of life. People of African descent wanted to go to war because they wished to live as free men and women with full rights and privileges in the land of their birth.

II

FIGHTING FOR A CHANCE TO FIGHT

*The North came slowly and reluctantly to rec-
ognize the Negro as a factor for good in the
war.*

CHRISTIAN A. FLEETWOOD,
Sergeant major, Fourth U.S. Colored Troops

Milton M. Holland was a seventeen-year-old schoolboy in Athens County, Ohio, in 1861. When the war
began, the state of Ohio asked for volunteers to join
the Union cause. Holland, like many other boys, decided to leave his schoolbooks for what he thought
would be the adventure of army life.

In April 1861, Holland went to the local army
recruiting station and offered his services. He was
told that he was too young to join; he was also rejected because he was black.

Milton Holland was a determined, patriotic
youngster. Since the army would not accept him, he
requested a job in the quartermaster's department
of the Ohio Volunteer Infantry. Holland received the
job. He couldn't enlist in the army, but he was able
to work for the military as a civilian.

Holland absorbed everything he could about military life while performing the mundane tasks of unloading supply wagons and handing out rations and

supplies to the soldiers. No doubt, he dreamed of one day proudly wearing the Union blue.

Isaac J. Hill, from Philadelphia, was another young man of African descent who waited for the time when he could become a soldier. Hill was ambitious and determined to go beyond the limitations placed on him because of his color. In 1861, however, all he could do was wait.

There were some men of color who were able to join Northern army regiments. Some, because they were light-skinned and passed for white, could enlist. Some Northern blacks, like Milton Holland, worked as laborers and servants in individual white regiments.

Black groups continued to petition the government to accept the enlistment of black soldiers, and in spite of the military's continued refusal, black men in several Northern cities formed military companies.[1] They believed that the time would come when the army would need their services. They, like young Milton Holland and Isaac J. Hill, waited for their time.

Frederick Douglass, too, waited and wondered how long Abraham Lincoln and his administration would insist that the war was not about slavery. Northern people of color waited impatiently for the federal government to accept the reality that the war *was* about slavery, and that blacks should be allowed to help the Union put an end to American slavery.

On the Southern front the mass of enslaved people did not wait for Lincoln to free them. They too had heard the shots fired on Fort Sumter, and they knew that the Yankees were fighting the people who held them in bondage. Many ignored their masters and mistresses who warned them to stay away from the Yankees—dangerous devils with tails who would kill them.

What would later become a great tidal wave of enslaved people taking freedom with their own hands started as a little ripple in a stream. The ripple appeared on a warm May evening in 1861, near Norfolk, Virginia, one month after Fort Sumter.

Three black men had just completed their work in the Confederate army camp. They, along with other men of African descent, dug trenches, built low walls for defense, erected and repaired bridges, constructed buildings, buried the dead, cleaned, cooked, and took care of the horses and mules that pulled the caissons. They did all of the fatigue duty that would normally be performed by the soldiers.

The three men had learned that the devilish Yankees were encamped in a nearby fort, perhaps they'd seen the Stars and Stripes flying over the fort. They probably didn't know about Lincoln's statements that the war wasn't being fought to end slavery. Yet they did know a lot about what was happening from conversations overheard among the soldiers and officers in the camp. The three men also had access to the great black "telegraph" whereby information traveled from person to person and from plantation to plantation.

The most important thing they knew was that the Yankees were fighting the people who held them in slavery. That was all they needed to know. On that May night, as the soldiers sat around their camp fires, the three slipped out of the Confederate camp and headed to Fortress Monroe.

As they approached the fort the Union guard stopped them and asked what they wanted. They had escaped from the Confederate camp and sought refuge, they told him. The guard found an officer who took the men to General Benjamin Butler, the commander of the fort.

At first the general didn't know what to do. The government's policy was to return runaways to slavery. But here were three strong men who had been working for the enemy. They were valuable enemy property. Military rules stated that valuable enemy property or contraband could be seized. He could always use men for the never-ending fatigue duty, and the camp needed a bakery.

Butler allowed the men to remain at the fort and paid them to build a bakery. Butler's actions were controversial because the government had not stated that fugitives would be treated as enemy property. The general, though, got his bakery and started a flood.

By the end of July 1861, approximately one thousand fugitives had escaped to Fortress Monroe. The tidal wave was rising, but the Lincoln administration still insisted that the war was not about slavery.

Emma E. Edmonds, who was a nurse and spy for the Union army, described the "contrabands" that she saw when she visited Fortress Monroe in 1861. "We set about visiting the contrabands. They occupied a long row of board buildings near the fort. The men were employed in loading and unloading Government vessels, and the women were busily engaged in cooking and washing. . . . One bitter, stormy night, about eleven o'clock, a band of these poor fugitives numbering over forty, presented themselves at the picket line, for admittance to the federal camp, imploring protection . . . the contrabands were permitted to pass through."[2]

In South Carolina the Wilson family, like the fugitives who made their way to Fortress Monroe, freed themselves. They fled to the Union-controlled Sea Islands off the coast. An observer wrote: "There was a family named Wilson. . . . Three or four brothers had planned an escape from the interior to our lines; they finally decided that the youngest should stay and take care of the old mother; the rest, with

Not waiting for Abraham Lincoln
to free them, this group of
contrabands escaped to Union lines
and freed themselves.

their sister and her children, came in a 'dug-out' down one of the rivers."[3]

Robert Smalls also couldn't wait for President Lincoln to free him and made one of the best-known and daring escapes of the war. Smalls had worked for many years as a boat pilot in the Charleston Harbor and was an expert navigator. He and eight other black men were part of the crew of the Confederate gunboat the *Planter*. Smalls devised a plan of escape and discussed it with the other black crew members. Together they decided to deliver the *Planter*, themselves, and their families to the Yankees.

On May 13, 1862, at 4 A.M., after the captain and the white crew had left the ship, Smalls smuggled his family and the families of the other black crew members on board. With the Confederate flag flying, they sailed the ship past the harbor forts, giving each the usual steam-whistle salute. No one manning the forts thought that anything was unusual.

When the *Planter* had safely passed the last fort and was approaching the federal blockade, Smalls hoisted a white flag. At that point the gunners in the Confederate forts realized what had happened and fired on the *Planter*. It was too late. Robert Smalls, the other crewmen, and their families, were free. Smalls was able to deliver a valuable vessel to the federals and, in addition, give them useful descriptions of the harbor and Confederate movements there. Many runaways supplied the Union army and navy with information about Confederate plans, defenses, and troop movements after they escaped from Southern territory.

The tide of freedom-seekers kept rising. Wherever Union forces appeared in the South, people of African descent fled to them for freedom and protection. By the summer of 1861, the growing number of men, women, and children escaping to Union lines

The *Planter*, and
seaman Robert Smalls,
who used it in a daring
break for freedom

was probably surprising the government; however, events later that summer would rock the North and ultimately cause a change in federal policy.

Early in July 1861, the Union and Confederate armies were in the process of shifting and moving forces and supplies and preparing for a war that each side thought it would quickly win. The federal government began to blockade Southern ports. Robert E. Lee refused President Lincoln's offer to take command of the Union Army. The Confederates moved their capital from Montgomery, Alabama, to Richmond, Virginia.

Northern and Southern civic organizations raised money for the war effort. Southern women made dashing uniforms for their men. Northern women sewed beautiful regimental flags. Young men on both sides of the conflict dreamed of adventure and glory. Filled with patriotic Yankee pride or patriotic Rebel pride, they rushed to recruiting stations.

No real battles or serious fighting had occurred after the Fort Sumter attack. Some Americans were still deciding where their sympathies lay, for there were Northerners who sided with the Confederates and Southerners who remained loyal to the Union. For example, the western section of Virginia refused to follow the rest of the state in seceding from the federal government.

Rioting that broke out between secessionist and Union factions in Baltimore resulted in thirteen deaths. Skirmishes erupted between Union and Confederate troops in Virginia and Missouri, but the divided nation had not yet experienced the real horror of war.

However the turmoil, excitement, and almost carnival-like atmosphere of those hot July days ended on July 21, 1861 at Manassas Junction, Virginia, near a stream called Bull Run.

Picnickers came from Washington, D.C., with lunch baskets to watch their army defeat the Confederates, capture the Confederate capital in Richmond, and bring the Southerners back to their senses and back into the Union. The Southern boys marched happily along the Virginia roads fringed with yellow goldenrod to meet their Northern counterparts. They laughed, saying that they would whip the Yankees and be home in time for dinner.

The battle began at five in the morning, July 21, 1861, and ended that evening when Union troops—and the picnickers—fled in panic back to Washington. This was the first major battle of the war, the Battle of Bull Run. Union losses were 1,124 wounded, 460 dead, and 312 missing. The Confederates had 1,582 wounded, 387 dead, and 13 missing. Both sides had to face the frightening possibility that the war would not be over quickly.

The North realized that the South was a formidable foe and would not be easily beaten. One of its strengths was its ability to use slave labor. In a letter to the Montgomery *Advertiser*, November 6, 1861, a writer boasted that slavery "is really one of the most effective weapons employed against the Union by the South."[4] Frederick Douglass and other antislavery reformers and abolitionists also recognized the important economic resource provided by four million enslaved women, men and children. Douglass urged that Lincoln weaken Confederate strength by declaring all slaves free. "The simple way then, to put an end to the savage and desolating war now waged by the slaveholders, is to strike down slavery itself," he wrote.[5]

The reformers and some Republicans in the federal government tried to convince Lincoln that it was futile to fight a war without taking away the South's most crucial source of power. They kept pressuring

Lincoln to declare slavery illegal and to allow black men to join the army. The North needed soldiers, and some people—even army officers—began to see blacks as an untapped source of men. General Butler had learned the usefulness of the captive slave population at Fortress Monroe.

Horace Greeley, editor of the New York *Tribune*, published an editorial entitled "Prayer of Twenty Millions" on August 19, 1862. In it he criticized Lincoln's position, saying, "All attempts to put down the Rebellion and at the same time uphold its inciting cause [slavery] are preposterous and futile." In a response to Greeley, Lincoln reiterated his position that the goal of the war was to save the nation. "I would save the Union. I would save it the shortest way under the Constitution. . . . If I could save the Union without freeing any slave I would do it, and if I could save it by freeing all the slaves I would do it."[6]

The defeat at Bull Run gave the North much to consider: Southern strength, slavery as a moral issue, and the acceptance of soldiers of African descent, like Milton Holland and Isaac J. Hill and Frederick Douglass's sons, into the army. Black leaders used the defeat at Bull Run to continue to pressure the president to declare that the eradication of slavery was the most important issue of the war, and to accept men of African descent into the army.

Yet, even after Bull Run, Lincoln resisted challenging slavery and accepting black soldiers. The Southerners, however, who had always exploited African labor, made good use of their black captives.

III

WORKING FOR
THE REBELS

*Black hands piled up the sand-bags and
raised the batteries, which drove Anderson
out of Sumter. At Montgomery . . . [N]egroes
were being drilled for military duty.*

WILLIAM WELLS BROWN

While the Union army continued to refuse to enlist
soldiers of color, the Confederates had a different
attitude. After their success at Bull Run, the Southerners made even greater and more creative use of
the black population in their midst.

At the beginning of the war, sons of well-to-do
families were given personal slaves to take along to
war, so that they would continue to enjoy some of
the comforts of home. Some rich slaveholders
avoided the draft by sending enslaved men as re-
placements. There were times, too, when black men
replaced dead or wounded soldiers in emergency sit-
uations during a battle.

Some free black men volunteered to help the Confederates when the war started. The Native Guards
of New Orleans, a black militia composed of free
blacks and mulattoes, with its own captains and lieutenants, offered to serve in the Confederate army at

the beginning of the war. Though they were never officially mustered into the Confederate army, and didn't fight for them, their services were accepted.

The Native Guards were not the only free blacks to offer their services to the Confederates. A Charleston, South Carolina, newspaper reported that one hundred fifty free blacks offered to help put up redoubts (small temporary forts) along the coast. "At Nashville, Tennessee, April, 1861, a company of free Negroes offered their services to the Confederate government and at Memphis a recruiting office was opened."[1]

Why did these free men of color offer to help the Confederate government? One reason was the fear of impressment—being forced to work for the military. In many cases there was no choice. As soon as the war began, free blacks in the Confederate states were suspect and had to offer to help to avoid being met with violence. Impressment of free as well as enslaved blacks was instituted even before Bull Run. Six Confederate states passed laws that provided for the impressment of free blacks into labor battalions, and some Confederate states forced free blacks into slavery during the war.[2]

Another reason black men volunteered to help the Confederates was that they were doing what blacks had done since colonial times—taking part in America's wars in the hope of attaining personal freedom and political rights.

Most of the enslaved men serving with the Confederate forces had been subjected to impressment. In Florida, slave owners were paid for the use of their slaves. The Confederate president, Jefferson Davis, considered impressing twenty thousand captives and giving them their freedom after they'd served in the military.[3]

The governor of Tennessee was given permission

The South made full use of its enslaved population, as shown here mounting a Confederate cannon at an army camp fortification in Mississippi.

in June 1861 to accept into the state militia black males between the ages of fifteen and fifty. The men were to receive eight dollars a month, plus clothing and rations. The sheriff of each county in Tennessee was given the names of all black men who were eligible to enlist. If the county did not get enough of these eligible men to "volunteer," then the sheriff could impress them into service.[4]

Seventy free blacks enlisted in the Confederate army in Lynchburg, Virginia. Sixteen companies of free men of color marched through Augusta, Georgia, on their way to fight in Virginia. A newspaper in Baltimore claimed that all of the able-bodied men in the area of Williamsport, Virginia, were impressed for service in Richmond, and were given arms so that they could defend the city.[5]

As the war dragged on, the Confederate govern-

ment widened its draft. In 1862 all white males between the ages of eighteen and thirty-five were sub-
ject to being called-up. In September the age limit
was moved up to forty-five years. By 1864 all white
males between seventeen and fifty could be drafted.

In February 1862, the Confederate War Department sent a message to a general in the field author-
izing him to "impress slaves and free [N]egroes to
extend and complete fortifications in the Peninsula."
By October of the same year, Jefferson Davis wrote
to the governor of Virginia asking for 4,500 blacks to
build fortifications in Richmond, Virginia.[6]

It seems, however, that when there was a chance
for these men to flee to the Union lines, they did.
John Parker, who eventually escaped to the Union
side, described his feelings at the Battle of Bull Run.

> There were four colored men in our battery. I don't know how
> many there were in the others. . . . my work was to hand the balls
> and swab out the cannon. . . . The officers aimed this gun; we
> fired grape shot. . . . I felt bad all the time, and thought every
> minute my time would come; I felt so excited that I hardly knew
> what I was about, and felt worse than dead. We wish to our hearts
> that the Yankees would [win], and we would have run over to their
> side but our officers would have shot us if we made the attempt.[7]

In 1862, when the Union forces captured New
Orleans, the Native Guards welcomed the Yankee
troops. Benjamin Butler asked the Guards why they
had joined the Confederates at the start of the war.
They said that they offered their services to the
Southerners because they had hoped to gain equality
with whites; however, their real sympathies were
with the Union cause.[8]

Some Confederates wanted to enlist slaves to
serve as fighting soldiers. A resident of Georgia
wrote to the Confederate secretary of war, "recom-

mending freedom after the war was over to those who fought, compensation to their owners and the retention of the institution of slavery by continuing as slaves 'boys and women, and exempted . . . men.' "[9]

However, most military men and leaders in the Confederate government agreed with General Howell Cobb, who said, "Use all the Negroes you can get for all purposes for which you need them, but don't arm them."[10] The Southern arguments against using black men were the same as those offered by Northerners: blacks were an inferior race and, therefore, would not make good soldiers; blacks were too cowardly to fight; white troops would not fight alongside blacks. The Confederates also feared slave insurrections.

By the close of the war, when the South was taking a terrific beating, attitudes changed. General Robert E. Lee wrote a long letter to a Richmond senator urging the arming of blacks in order to fill the depleted ranks of white soldiers. "We must decide whether slavery shall be extinguished by our enemies and the slaves be used against us. . . . There have been formidable armies composed of men having no interest in the cause for which they fought beyond their pay or hope of plunder . . . such an interest we can give our Negroes by giving immediate freedom to all who enlist . . . together with the privilege of residing at the South. . . ."[11]

On March 13, 1865, the Confederate government passed a law allowing the enlistment of black soldiers in the Confederate army. "The President . . . is hereby authorized to ask for and accept from the owners of slaves, the services of . . . able-bodied Negro men . . . to perform military service in whatever capacity he may direct."[12] However, the war ended before large-scale black recruiting could begin.

This war between the North and South gave enslaved men and women an opportunity to take advantage of unstable conditions created by the warring whites. This was one way for some black people to initiate their march for their own freedom. Caught between two fires, they had to find a way to survive the conflict. And for some, one way to survive was to volunteer to help the Confederates.

The promise of freedom for themselves and their families was enough of an incentive to join the Confederate Army, and the Union had said that it was not fighting to end slavery.

IV

HUNTER'S REGIMENT

*The first suits worn by the boys were red coats
and pants, which they disliked very much, for,
they said, "The rebels see us, miles away."*

SUSIE KING TAYLOR

On May 9, 1862, a company of Union soldiers, muskets slung over their shoulders, carefully surveyed the large plantation with its dairy and spinning houses, smokehouse, and barns. They walked past a peach orchard, toward the live oak trees draped with gray moss. The trees lined a path that led to a large house with white columns gleaming in the sunlight.

Small cottages and cabins stood behind the big house. Old women sat on their rickety cabin porches watching children play. Beyond the cabins, cows grazed lazily. Fields, dotted with women and men tilling the soil, stretched as far as the eye could see. The soldiers quickened their pace as they marched toward the fields. "The general said that we should take only strong, healthy men who look like they can learn how to fire a musket," the officer leading the company said. Then they rushed into the field, the troops fanning out as if to form a net around the men and women.

The women screamed when they looked up from the ground and saw the soldiers pointing muskets at the young men and ordering them away from their work. Several men ran in the direction of the woods as the soldiers chased them, firing into the air. One woman begged the soldiers to allow her to bring her husband extra clothing before they took him away.

The children and women cried when they saw their fathers and husbands, sons and brothers, being led off the plantation by the troops. The women feared that they would never see their husbands again. The men thought that they were being taken away from their families to be sold into slavery in Cuba by the Yankee soldiers.

The men were not going to be sent to Cuba or reenslaved. They were being taken to General David Hunter who, like Frederick Douglass, Harriet Tubman, and even some of the Republicans in his own administration, was frustrated by Lincoln's reluctance to accept black men into the military.

Hunter, a West Point graduate and a staunch abolitionist, was an impatient man who was ready to take matters into his own hands. When he took command of the Department of the South on March 31, 1862, he found himself in a difficult situation. The department, a group of islands off the coasts of South Carolina, Georgia, and northern Florida, had been captured by Union forces in November 1861. The whites who owned the rich cotton and rice plantations had abandoned the Sea Islands and fled to the mainland when the Union army and navy arrived.[1] Many of the slaves who worked the plantations remained. In the following months, they were joined by thousands of black men, women, and children who escaped to the islands from the mainland.

General Hunter's problem was that he did not

Freed blacks worked the cotton plantations
of the Sea Islands.

have enough soldiers to maintain control of the tidal
rivers and all the islands that made up the area.
He needed more soldiers, but there would be none
coming. Union armies were heavily engaged else-
where and could not be spared to reinforce the department.

Hunter's situation was bleak. The Union needed
to continue to hold Port Royal Harbor so that it could
blockade the Atlantic and capture Charleston. The
federal troops just barely controlled the Sea Islands
and were constantly plagued by guerrilla forces—

bands of armed Confederates who raided and harassed the Union troops in order to regain the islands. Hunter's predecessor, General Thomas W. Sherman, had been given permission by the War Department to arm the blacks on the islands "if special circumstances seem to require it."[2] Sherman had not armed them, but organized the former plantation slaves and the fugitives from the mainland, and settled them on the abandoned plantations to grow cotton and rice for the Treasury Department.

They were now neither slave nor free. They had no rights under the Constitution because they were not citizens of the United States, even though most of them had been born in America. Hunter, surveying his new command, saw one way out of his problem. Deciding that the circumstances were "special," and under the authorization given Sherman, Hunter proceeded to recruit the fugitives and former slaves into the army.

On April 13 he took an important step without the president's permission. He declared that "All persons held as slaves on Cockspur Island, Georgia, and in Fort Pulaski by enemies of the United States are hereby confiscated and declared free."[3]

Basing his declaration on the First Confiscation Act, he ordered his commanders in the field to recruit blacks into the army.[4] Then, on May 8, Hunter took another step without permission of the president or the War Department. He announced that "The persons in these three states, Georgia, Florida and South Carolina, heretofore held as slaves are therefore declared forever free."[5] Of course his decree had no impact on slavery in mainland Georgia, Florida, or South Carolina where the Confederates were in control. He then ordered his commanders "to send immediately to these headquarters under a guard all the able-bodied [N]egroes capable of bearing arms."[6]

46

Unfortunately, Hunter's impatience worked against him. He did not wait for volunteers and his good intentions were almost ruined when black men were forced by local commanders to join the army. The men were not given time to volunteer. No one explained that they could enlist if they chose to.

In spite of this poor beginning, Hunter was able to start to form a regiment. Once the men found out that they were not to be sold into slavery, quite a number joined voluntarily. One volunteer was a man named Prince Rivers, who had escaped captivity in Beaufort, South Carolina, and sought refuge with the Yankees.

When there were enough men, one company was formed—Company A, led by Captain Trowbridge. Rivers and the other recruits in Company A were given uniforms of red pantaloons and braided jackets instead of the regular Union blue.

Newspapers reported daily on Hunter's efforts to raise a regiment. Many reporters scoffed at the idea that blacks would fight and ridiculed the soldiers in their red pantaloons. Other reporters wrote that fugitives were hiding and that men were being cruelly snatched from plantations and fields. A *New York Times* report, however, said they performed excellently during drill "with a silent obedience and accuracy hardly to be surpassed by any white regiment at Hilton Head."[7]

News did not travel as quickly in those days and in June, when President Lincoln and the War Department finally got wind of General Hunter's activities through the newspapers and letters from the superintendents of the plantations complaining about the enlistment of their workers, the president wrote an angry letter to the general. He informed Hunter that neither he nor any other general had the right to declare anyone free. Hunter sent an angry and emotional reply to the War Department, explaining his need for black regiments. The tone of his letter offended the War Department and some members of Congress. Hunter, they said, was an ultra-abolitionist who should not be given the delicate task of raising a black regiment.[8]

Without official authority to form a regiment, Hunter was forced to disband it on August 10, 1862. It was a sad day for Hunter and for Prince Rivers and the other men of Company A. Hunter may have felt that he had failed, but his bold efforts initiated a movement that would lead to the acceptance of men of African descent into the army.

Christian A. Fleetwood, a black man who later was able to enlist, said, "To General David Hunter more than to any other one man, is due the credit for the successful entry . . . of the Negro as a soldier in this war."[9]

Two weeks after Hunter regretfully dismissed the men, the War Department gave General Rufus Saxton permission to raise a black regiment. Out of the remnants of "Hunter's Regiment" came the First South Carolina Volunteers, led by Colonel Thomas Wentworth Higginson. This was the first black regiment to be mustered into the Union army. The First Kansas Colored Volunteers was also organized at about this time, but without War Department sanction. It was officially mustered into the army after the First South Carolina Volunteers.

The South Carolina regiment received a great deal of attention both from people who thought that the "experiment" to arm black men would be a failure, and from those who sincerely wanted it to succeed.

When several companies of the regiment made their first military expedition, General Saxton

President Abraham Lincoln reveals the Emancipation
Proclamation to his cabinet, July 22, 1862.

warned Colonel Higginson not to take too many risks for fear of swaying public opinion against the black troops. That first expedition and others in the Sea Islands were very successful. One reason for the regiment's successes was that men, including Prince Rivers and others from the region, provided the officers with valuable information about navigation; the terrain; places where lumber, food, and other valuable supplies might be foraged; and places where Confederate guerrillas might hide. The First South Carolina and other black regiments that organized later in the coastal areas were instrumental also in defending and holding the Sea Islands and other regions in the Department of the South.

On July 17, 1862, Lincoln signed the Second Confiscation Act and a militia act that provided for the use of black soldiers and the emancipation of soldiers and their families if their former masters were Confederates.[10] Slowly, the first steps were being taken toward emancipation and the inclusion of blacks in the military. But for Frederick Douglass and other black leaders, and the voiceless mass of black people who were freeing themselves, and for the abolitionists and even for the president's Republican Party, these measures were not enough. Slavery—the real cause of the war—had to be eliminated. Lincoln finally agreed. On July 22, 1862, he revealed his Emancipation Proclamation to his cabinet, and then tried to figure out what would be done with four million freed Africans in a reunified United States once the war was over.

Lincoln was advised to issue his proclamation from a position of strength—to wait until the Union had won a military victory. In September 1862 the Union forces, at great cost, won the Antietam Campaign and President Abraham Lincoln issued his Emancipation Proclamation.

WHO WILL LEAD?

Let an officer be only just and firm with a cordial, kindly nature, and he has no sort of difficulty.

THOMAS WENTWORTH HIGGINSON

January 1, 1863, was a day of celebration for blacks throughout the North—the day of jubilee. Meetings were held in churches throughout the North. Frederick Douglass attended a large jubilee celebration at Tremont Temple in Boston that night. Lincoln had signed the Emancipation Proclamation. Even though the document did not free people held in slavery in the loyal border states, or in Confederate areas that were still loyal to the Union, the crowd was ecstatic.[1] Because of the proclamation, people held in bondage who came into Union lines would be free. The document also allowed for men of African descent to join the military.

A few weeks after the Emancipation Proclamation was signed, the War Department began the process of recruiting men and officers for the black regiments. Finally Milton Holland, now nineteen years old, could join the military. In June 1863 he

"Come and Join Us, Brothers"
was the headline on this
recruiting poster for black soldiers.

was mustered into the Union army and became a
private in the Fifth U.S. Colored Troops—an Ohio
regiment. Isaac J. Hill enlisted in the Twenty-ninth
Regiment of Connecticut Colored Troops. Frederick
Douglass's two sons joined the Fifty-fourth Massachusetts, Christian A. Fleetwood joined the Fourth
U.S. Colored Troops, and all of the other men of color
who wanted to were able to enlist in the Union army.

Now, the great experiment began. Except for
some people in the military, and the abolitionists, it
seemed that only black people themselves believed
that men of African descent would be successful soldiers. Many Americans seemed to have little faith
in the black soldier's ability to follow instructions,
accept discipline, and fight. Some thought blacks

were cowards and would run at the sight of Confederate soldiers pointing guns in their direction. Americans who were anti-black were sure that the experiment would be a failure, but the black soldiers and their supporters were determined that it would be a success. Black people had not forgotten that soldiers of color had fought in the Revolutionary War and the War of 1812. They knew that if given a chance, they'd become as fine soldiers as other men.

The first recruits for the black regiments were the officers—all of whom were white. Because of continued resistance to allowing black men into the army, and to reassure those who were predicting failure, the War Department ruled that all the officers of the black regiments were to be white.

The ability of black men to function as soldiers was so mistrusted that it was felt that the most highly qualified white men were needed to lead them. Edward M. Main, an officer in a black regiment, believed that black troops were successful in the army because they had competent white officers. Further, black officers would have been entitled to the same rights and respect enjoyed by white officers. This was unthinkable in nineteenth-century America.

Since the War Department wanted to be sure that the white men selected would be excellent officers, it instituted—for the first time in United States military history—an examining board to review officers of black troops. Major General Silas Casey was president of the board. "We consider alone in making our awards, the ability of the person to serve his country in the duties pertaining to the office," he said, adding that if the board felt that the applicant did not have enough knowledge or skills he would be rejected.[2]

The War Department also established the Bureau of Colored Troops to oversee the administration of the black regiments, or the United States Colored Troops (USCT), as they were officially called. The Bureau provided information, supervised the recruitment of men and officers, gathered supplies, and handled a vast amount of paperwork, supervising approximately 186,000 officers and men.[3]

Some of the officers were distinguished men. A number came from abolitionist and Republican families and were, by nineteenth-century standards, well educated. George Thompson Garrison, son of William Lloyd Garrison, was an officer in the Fifty-fifth Massachusetts (Colored) Infantry. Charles Francis Adams, Jr., grandson of President John Quincy Adams, served in the Fifth Massachusetts (Colored) Cavalry; Robert Gould Shaw, the son of a wealthy abolitionist, led the Massachusetts Fifty-fourth Regiment. William Birney, son of the abolitionist James Gillespie Birney, organized seven black regiments. James Chaplin Beecher, the half brother of the abolitionist writer Harriet Beecher Stowe, was also an officer in one of the black regiments. Thomas Wentworth Higginson, an abolitionist minister, served as a colonel leading the First South Carolina Volunteers.

Charlotte Forten, a free black Northern schoolteacher who taught in the Sea Islands during the Civil War, described both Colonel Higginson and Colonel Shaw in her journals.

[Higginson] seems to me of all fighting men the one best fitted to command a regiment of colored soldiers. . . . we used to see Higginson drilling his white company. I never saw him so full of life and energy—entering with his whole soul into his work—without thinking what a splendid general he [would] make. . . .

I am perfectly charmed with Colonel Shaw. He seems to me in every way one of the most delightful persons I have ever met.

There is something girlish about him, and yet I never saw anyone more manly. To me he seems a thoroughly lovable person. . . . The perfect breeding, how evident it is. . . .[4]

Civilians and military men were able to apply for a commission with the USCT. A soldier could get a letter of recommendation from the commanding officer of his volunteer unit. Civilians needed letters from well-known and respected citizens. After submitting letters of recommendation, the candidates were given verbal examinations in which they were questioned by the examining board on their knowledge of military tactics, arithmetic, geography, and history.

When General Hunter was trying to raise his regiment in South Carolina, he said that he wanted officers who were intelligent, experienced, moral, and willing to help the black race. Thomas Wentworth Higginson, who later commanded Hunter's old regiment, said that he wanted only officers who cared about blacks, and who were bright and respectable. When Governor Andrew of Massachusetts was searching for someone to command the Fifty-Fourth Massachusetts, he said that he was looking for young men who had "firm anti-slavery principles. . . . Such officers must necessarily be gentlemen of the highest tone and honor."[5]

Quite a few of the men who received commissions in the USCT believed that they and their fellow officers were superior to officers in white regiments because of the stringent selection standards. A USCT officer claimed that—with money—anyone could get a commission in a white regiment, but that was not the case in the USCT.[6]

In spite of the selection process, not every officer was a committed abolitionist, nor highly intelligent and moral. Most of the officers in the USCT were Republicans and had fought in the war from the very

beginning. They did not all come from abolitionist families, and most had joined the army not to fight slavery, but to support their president and government.

A commission with the USCT was a way for an enlisted man to become an officer, and an officer's life was easier than that of a soldier. Officers earned $120 a month, while enlisted men received $13 a month. Some men who tried but couldn't get promotions in their white volunteer units found it easier to get promotions in the USCT.

Though officers were supposedly carefully screened, no examination is infallible. Some unsuitable men did get commissions and there were instances where politicians awarded commissions as a way to grant favors to supporters and friends.[7]

There were also instances where officers were cruel and harsh to the men they were supposed to lead, and there were incompetent officers who were unable to train and discipline the men. Prejudice was so deeply rooted in the North that many officers had to shed false notions and myths about black inferiority before they could be effective leaders.

A few officers had absolutely no regard or respect for the soldiers, and even attempted to steal their money. Sometimes the soldiers received large sums of back pay. Men who had families in the North could send their money home; however, men who had escaped from slavery could not send their money to

Colonel Robert Gould Shaw
(central figure, at top),
photographed in 1859 with
the First Virginia Regiment,
became the leader of the
Massachusetts Fifty-fourth Regiment.

families who were still captives in the South. Sometimes these men gave the money to their officers to hold for them.

One captain in the 9th U.S. Colored Infantry tried to resign from the company after his troops gave him their money for safekeeping. A lieutenant in the 2nd U.S. Colored Infantry also tried to resign while holding two thousand dollars for his troops. The War Department forced him to return the money.[8]

But for the most part the USCT officers were competent men, sharing the danger as well as the limited credit given to the USCT troops. Selecting officers was just the beginning of a difficult job. As soon as some of the officers for a regiment were designated, the hard work of recruiting the men began.

VI

CALL TO ARMS

Once let the black man get upon his person the brass letters, U.S.; let him get an eagle on his button, and a musket on his shoulder and bullets in his pocket, and there is no power on earth which can deny that he has earned the right to citizenship in the United States.

FREDERICK DOUGLASS

When General Joseph Hooker took command of the Army of the Potomac in January 1863, he informed the War Department that 85,123 officers and men were AWOL (absent without leave); that many of the units did not have enough clothing, food, or adequate shelter; and that troop morale was low.[1] The conflict was entering its second year and Northerners were war-weary. Yet, despite all these factors, some people were still against accepting black men into the military.

One officer told the president that "A decided majority of our officers of all grades have no sympathy with your policy. . . . They hate the Negro more than they love the Union." A Union colonel expressed his dissatisfaction with the Emancipation Proclamation and Lincoln's policy, saying he feared that the loyal border states would leave the Union and join the Confederacy. However, as the lists of dead and wounded grew, the idea of a new source of manpower became more appealing, especially in villages and towns where every family had suffered the loss of a father or a son.

Most of the Civil War regiments were raised by states. Some states had trouble meeting their draft quotas, but once they could draft men of African descent, they were able to fulfill them.

John Andrew, the governor of Massachusetts, had long advocated the use of blacks in the military. When he received permission from the War Department on January 26, 1863, to recruit "persons of African descent, organized into special corps," he immediately named officers for a proposed black regiment and began to recruit men from his state, before the government's policy could change.[2] This regiment would become the Fifty-fourth Massachusetts Infantry.

A captain in the regiment, Luis F. Emilio, wrote in his regimental history that "Early in February quite a number of colored men were recruited in Philadelphia. . . ." He noted that it was difficult to recruit there because they virtually had to sneak the men out of Philadelphia in small groups, so that they would not be harassed by whites. "The gathering-place had to be kept secret, and the men sent to Massachusetts in small parties to avoid molestation or excitement." The Massachusetts recruiting agent had "to purchase railroad tickets himself, and get the recruits one at a time on the cars under cover of darkness."[3]

Recruiting in Bedford, Massachusetts, was easier. Black ministers of that city opened the doors of their churches for recruitment meetings. Frederick Douglass, William Lloyd Garrison, Wendell Phillips and other prominent leaders addressed meetings. Black leaders—William Wells Brown, Charles L. Remond, John Mercer Langston, Henry Highland Garnet, Martin R. Delaney, and Frederick Douglass—were hired by the government to recruit throughout the North and in Canada for enlistees for the Fifty-fourth Massachusetts Infantry. Douglass's sons, Charles and Lewis, were the first recruits from New York State to join the regiment. A committee of prominent white citizens was also instrumental in raising money and recruiting for the Fifty-fourth. By May enough men had volunteered for the regiment so that a second black Massachusetts regiment, The Fifty-fifth Massachusetts Infantry, was organized.

Rhode Island had a history of accepting black soldiers. A black regiment had been raised there during the American Revolution. As early as August 1862, the governor of Rhode Island was prepared to raise a regiment from his state that would "consist entirely of colored citizens." The order that authorized the governor to raise the regiment stated "Our Colored fellow-citizens are reminded that the Regiment from this State in the Revolution, consisting entirely of colored persons, was pronounced by [George] Washington equal, if not superior, to any in the service. . . ."[4]

According to William H. Chenery, in his history of the Fourteenth Rhode Island Heavy Artillery (Colored), the black people of Rhode Island held public meetings to discuss raising a black regiment and that about one hundred men enrolled. Since it was not clear to state leaders whether the black volunteers would be soldiers or laborers, the regiment was not formed. By 1863, when another draft was held and the state quota had to be filled, there was little white resistance to raising a black regiment.[5] The regiment left for service on December 19, 1863.

The governors of Connecticut, Maryland, and

Pennsylvania also began to form black regiments in their states. On June 17, 1863, just before the Battle of Gettysburg, a company of black men "appeared at the city arsenal and applied for uniforms and guns. They were fitted without question. . . ."[6] It seems as if the color of the men volunteering was less troubling when danger was imminent. Eleven regiments were mustered in at Camp William Penn in Philadelphia.

In Kansas, Brigadier General Jim Lane ignored the War Department's warnings in 1862 that he had no authorization to form a regiment. His troops saw combat and then were officially mustered into the army in January 1863.

Horatio Seymour, the governor of New York, showed little interest in raising a black regiment in his state. In July 1863, anti-black violence erupted in New York City. The rioters were mostly immigrants who resented being called for the draft, feeling that they were being asked to fight for blacks. Their anger against the draft enrollment office turned to rage against the city's black population. For four days, "Dozens of Negroes were lynched in the streets or murdered in their homes. The Colored Orphan Asylum was burned to the ground."[7] Many New York residents were so distressed by the incident that they raised money to rebuild the orphanage.

The situation in New York was considered so dangerous that the governor of Massachusetts was advised on July 9, 1863, "not to send the Fifty-fifth Massachusetts Colored Regiment through this city, on their way to the seat of war, because the lives of colored women and children here would be endangered."[8]

However, the Union League Club—a group of wealthy white New Yorkers—wrote to the governor and the War Department on November 27, 1863,

Draft protesters rioted in New York City.

asking for permission to raise a black regiment. "On behalf of the Union League Club of this city we respectfully ask an authorization for a regiment of Colored Troops, to be raised in the State of New York. . . ." The letter then stated that the club "is composed of over five hundred of the wealthiest and most respectable citizens of New York . . ." who are loyal to the government and have already promised a large sum of money for raising the regiment. They wanted to put into "the field a regiment worthy to stand side by side with the Fifty-fourth of Massachusetts."[9]

The League was given permission on December 3, 1863, to provide money for a black regiment from New York—the Twentieth Regiment United States Colored Troops. The men were trained and quartered at Rikers Island in New York's East River.

Recruitment in New York was difficult. Because of prejudice inside and outside the military, black New Yorkers were reluctant to join. Henry Highland Garnet, who had been demanding, along with other black leaders, that black men should be allowed to join the army, spoke against black enlistment at a New York recruiting meeting in April 1863, because black soldiers would not receive the same pay as white soldiers and could not become officers.

However, at a larger New York meeting a few days later, Frederick Douglass stated that even though he was angered by the government policy, joining the army was one way for blacks to prove that they were the equal of white men. Justice would be attained once the war against slavery was won, he counseled. "Action! Action! Not criticism," he said.[10]

Recruiting was even more frustrating—and at times dangerous—in the border states (where the Emancipation Proclamation did not apply), and in Confederate territories captured by the Union.

J. M. Califf, a first lieutenant serving with the Seventh Regiment of U.S. Colored Troops, wrote about his recruiting experiences in Maryland. Recruiting for the regiment began on October 29, 1863. After two weeks, the regiment had five hundred men. Califf said that the officers recruiting for the regiment were told to "raid through the country, carrying off slaves from under the eyes of their masters."

However, carrying off a slave from under the eyes of a master could be dangerous. Another Seventh Regiment officer, a Lieutenant White, found out that a Confederate colonel was holding black men captive in his house so that they couldn't enlist. The lieutenant went to the colonel's house and ordered him and his son to free the men, but they refused. The lieutenant then went to the fields where other enslaved men were working in an attempt to enlist them in the Seventh Regiment. The colonel and his son followed Lieutenant White and shot and killed him.[11]

There were some times when Califf and other officers met with no resistance from slave owners. He visited a large plantation near Caperville, Virginia, and asked the owner to call his slaves. The man agreed. "As we started to walk away the old man turned to me and with tears in his eyes said, 'Will you take them all? Here I am an old man, I cannot work; my crops are ungathered; my Negroes have all enlisted or run away. What am I to do?' "[12]

Sometimes recruiting was very slow. In a journal entry dated July 29, 1864, John Ayers, who was recruiting in Alabama, wrote: "Just returned from a scout of two days Down to White burg, had ten Colored troops with me armed. Brought in five Recruits. . . . I got some 15 men but some was Lame some Ruptured some pane in back some Rumatism some toothache and so on till five was all the net of my trip."[13]

There were instances when field commanders did not want to lose the men who had been working for the army as laborers, so they discouraged them from joining as soldiers. Lincoln told one commander that he must comply with the law and allow men who wanted to enlist to leave their work as laborers for the military.

Brigadier General Lorenzo Thomas was sent by Secretary of War Edwin Stanton to organize recruitment in the Mississippi Valley. He was instrumental in raising fifty black regiments—from Alabama, Arkansas, Florida, Kentucky, Iowa, Louisiana, Mississippi, and Tennessee—with an approximate total of fifty thousand men. By the fall of 1864, 140 black regiments had been raised.[14]

The experiment was well on its way.

VII

THE MEN

*If slaves make good soldiers, our whole theory
of slavery is wrong.*

CONFEDERATE GENERAL HOWELL COBB

Milton Holland, Christian A. Fleetwood, and all the
other black volunteers were watched closely by the
American public. Any mistakes or failures on the
part of the USCT were seen as proof—to those who
did not want blacks in the army—that they were not
fit to be soldiers. The soldiers of the USCT knew that
they had to be better than average white soldiers in
order to gain even a small amount of respect.

Colonel Higginson said that his regiment lived
for months in a glare of publicity. A steady stream
of visitors—military as well as civilian—came to the
camp. "I felt sometimes," Higginson wrote, "as if we
were a plant trying to take root, but constantly
pulled up to see if we were growing. The slightest
camp incidents sometimes came back to us, magnified and distorted, in letters of anxious inquiry from
remote parts of the Union. It was no pleasant thing
to live under such constant surveillance."[1]

Who were the men who filled the ranks of the black regiments? In official documents they are represented by numbers and labels: Contraband, ex-slaves, slaves, freeborn, freedmen, fugitives, blacks, Africans, Negroes, Coloreds. Most importantly, they were men. More than 75,000 from the Northern states volunteered. Some had escaped slavery and welcomed the chance first to work for the army for wages, and then to fight for the army when allowed to enlist.[2]

In the South, too, there were men who volunteered. Others were conscripted (drafted) when Confederate territory was captured by the Union army. The federal government recruited approximately 99,000 men through volunteer enlistments and through conscription in the South.[3]

There were men like William H. Carney, who became a sergeant in the Massachusetts Fifty-fourth. He was a twenty-two-year-old seaman from New Bedford, Massachusetts, when he joined the regiment. Carney won the Congressional Medal of Honor for saving the flag at Fort Wagner, South Carolina, where he suffered wounds.

There was Peter Vogelsang, the quartermaster sergeant of the Massachusetts Fifty-fourth, who eventually became a second lieutenant despite War Department opposition to allowing black men to become commissioned officers. Vogelsang was forty-six years old, married, and working as a printer in Brooklyn, New York, when he volunteered.

Lewis H. Douglass, a son of Frederick Douglass, became a sergeant major in the Massachusetts Fifty-fourth. When he joined the regiment he was twenty-two years old and worked as a printer in Rochester, New York.

Samuel Sufshay, a drummer in the Massachusetts Fifty-fourth, was seventeen years old when he was killed by a mortar shell.

An 1864 engraving shows a black Union soldier.

Black officers of the
Massachusetts Fifty-fourth Regiment.
Bottom left: Lieutenant Stephen A.
Swails. Top right: Lieutenant Frank
M. Welch. Bottom right: Lieutenant
Peter Vogelsang.

Stephen A. Swails was a thirty-year-old married boatman from Elmira, New York. By the end of the war, he had been commissioned as a second lieutenant in the Massachusetts Fifty-fourth.

In the Massachusetts Fifty-fifth there were men like carpenter John F. Shorter, age twenty-one, from Delaware. He became a sergeant and was wounded in the battle for Honey Hill, South Carolina, in 1864. William H. Dupree, age twenty-five, was a plasterer from Ohio. He became a sergeant and was promoted to second lieutenant in 1865.

Corporal Robert King was an eighteen-year-old farmer from Ohio when he joined the regiment. William Wells Brown described him as "the young, the handsome and the gentlemanly sergeant, whose youth and bravery attract the attention of all."[4] King was the color bearer for the regiment and was killed in the battle for Honey Hill. The regiment also had a seaman from Africa, William Williams. He was forty years old when he joined the regiment in January 1864, and he died of typhoid fever on August 19, 1864.

The regiments raised in the South also had an interesting array of men. One was André Callioux, who called himself the blackest man in New Orleans. At forty years of age, he was one of the leaders of that city's free black community. He'd been educated in Paris and could read and write English and French. Callioux was a wealthy family man, and is described as being respected by whites and blacks in New Orleans. He was an officer in the First Louisiana Native Guards, then raised a company of black soldiers and offered its support to the Union army.[5]

John Crowder was also an officer in the Native Guards. He too had always been free, but was not as wealthy as Callioux. He worked hard from the time he was a youngster in order to help support his mother. Crowder had been a steward on a Mississippi steamboat, and had also worked as a porter for a jeweler. Schooling was important to him and his mother, and along with his hard work, he struggled to gain an education from a black clergyman.

Crowder had lied about his age in order to join the Native Guards and became, possibly, the youngest officer in the Union army. "If Abraham Lincoln knew that a colored Lad of my age could command a company what would he say?"[6] He may have been as young as sixteen or seventeen when he became a lieutenant in the Native Guards.

In the First South Carolina Volunteers (the regiment started by General Hunter in the Sea Islands), there were men like Prince Rivers. Rivers and his fellow soldiers were called contraband because they had been the human "property" of the enemy. They had escaped slavery, but were not quite free, either, as non-citizens of what had been the United States.

Colonel Higginson described Rivers glowingly as

Our color-sergeant, who is provost-sergeant also, and has entire charge of the prisoners and of the daily policing of the camp. He is a man of distinguished appearance, and in old times was the crack coachman of Beaufort. . . . They tell me that he was once allowed to present a petition to the Governor of South Carolina in behalf of slaves . . . and that a placard offering two thousand dollars for his recapture is still to be seen by the wayside between here and Charleston.

He was a sergeant in the old 'Hunter Regiment' and was taken by General Hunter to New York last spring, where the chevrons on his arm brought a mob upon him in Broadway, whom he kept off till the police interfered. There is not a white officer in this regiment who has more administrative ability, or more absolute authority over the men; they do not love him, but his mere presence has controlling power over them.

> He writes well enough to prepare for me a daily report of his duties in the camp; if his education reached a higher point, I see no reason why he should not command the Army of the Potomac . . . . his complexion, like that of others of my darkest men, having a sort of rich, clear depth . . . and to my eye very handsome. . . .[7]

Higginson added that Rivers was six feet tall and had a physique "superior to that of any of our white officers." Higginson also described another man in his regiment: "Corporal Robert Sutton . . . if not in all respects the ablest, he was the wisest man in our ranks. As large, and as powerful and as black as our good-looking Color sergeant, but more heavily built. . . ." Though he could neither read nor write, Higginson explained, he was extremely intelligent and wanted "intellectual companionship. . . . He was a Florida man, and had been chiefly employed in lumbering and piloting on the St. Mary's River, which divides Florida from Georgia. Down this stream he had escaped in a 'dug-out,' " and after he found his way to the Union camp, he returned to Florida to bring his wife and child out of slavery and to the safety of one of the settlements near the First South Carolina Regiment camp that had been set up for fugitives from slavery. Robert Sutton was not the only man in the regiment who risked returning to Confederate territory to help his family escape to freedom. Other men in the regiment did the same.[8]

Prince Rivers and Robert Sutton also impressed Charlotte Forten, the black schoolteacher from the North. She was at the camp on New Year's Day, 1863, for the Emancipation Day celebration there: "I thought I had never seen a sight so beautiful . . . the black soldiers, in their blue coats and scarlet pants, the officers of this and other regiments in their handsome uniforms and crowds of lookers-on. . . . Prince

Despite barriers and prejudice,
many black soldiers in the
United States Colored Troops—
including this Union corporal—
proved their leadership ability.

Rivers and Robert Sutton made very good speeches
indeed, and were loudly cheered."[9]

Isaac J. Hill, a private in the Twenty-ninth Regiment of Connecticut Colored Troops, was one of the
few enlisted black men who left a written record of
his service in the army. Hill was a proud and religious man who took a firm stand protesting the lower
pay received by black troops.

A Providence, Rhode Island, newspaper described the Fourteenth Rhode Island Heavy Artillery
(Colored):

The appearance of three hundred muskets in our streets in the hands of as many sturdy, stalwart black men, was a novel sight in Providence. . . . Peter, the file leader, is a splendidly formed man, huge, muscular and powerfully built. Charles Freeman is his equal. Peter is from the border [one of the southern states bordering the north] and from slavery. Charles is of Rhode Island stock and hails from Bristol. Jeremiah Noka . . . is also a noteworthy specimen of a Rhode Islander. [Noka, like a number of black Rhode Islanders, was of mixed heritage—African and Narragansett Indian.] His fine shape, his decided Indian cast of features, his genial and winning smile . . . recall the memory of the lost Narragansetts. Sergeants Jenkins, Phenix, and Howland, of this city, are well known and capable men, and well drilled soldiers.[10]

Edward M. Main, a major of the Third United States Colored Cavalry, organized in Tennessee, wrote that the soldiers in his regiment had been recruited from the men who had already been working as servants, teamsters, cooks, hostlers, and laborers for the Union army. "The enlisted men were far above the average of those in [other] colored regiments," he bragged. "Having thousands of likely young colored men to choose from, none but the finest specimens of physical manhood were accepted, care being taken to enlist none but young, active men, of medium weight, regard also being had to a fair amount of natural intelligence. Physically, therefore, the enlisted men of the regiment approached as near to that standard of ideal cavalrymen as has probably ever been realized. . . . They were superb horsemen," and adjusted quickly and easily to military life. "They soon become proficient in all the duties of a soldier."[11] General Ulysses S. Grant, Main said, decided to raise a USCT regiment of cavalry at Vicksburg. It was called the First Mississippi Cavalry, African Descent. The name was changed to Third

United States Colored Cavalry. Main said that in six months the regiment was complete, "and stood on an equal footing with the veteran cavalry of the department. . . . During that period the regiment had taken an active part in many important expeditions and had participated in numerous engagements, and suffered a loss of many killed and wounded."[12]

Thomas J. Morgan, the colonel for the Fourteenth United States Colored Infantry, evidently did not have the same choice of men as the organizers of the Third United States Colored Cavalry did:

> There were at that time several hundred [N]egro men in camp, in charge of, I think, a lieutenant. They were a motley crowd—old, young, middle-aged. Some wore the United States uniform, but most of them had on the clothes in which they had left the plantations, or had worn during periods of hard service as laborers in the army. Gallatin [Tennessee] at that time was threatened with an attack by the guerrilla bands then prowling over that part of the State. General Paine had issued a hundred old muskets and rifles to the [N]egroes in camp. They had not passed a medical examination, had no company organization, and had had no drill. Almost immediately upon my arrival, as an attack was imminent, I was ordered to distribute another hundred muskets, and to "prepare every available man for fight."
>
> In the course of a few weeks, however, we had a thousand able-bodied, stalwart men. . . . I found that a considerable number of them had been teamsters, cooks, officers' servants, etc., and had thus seen a good deal of hard service in both armies, in camp, on the march, and in battle, and so knew pretty well what to expect.[13]

The men of this regiment then, had experienced the war at firsthand before joining the army, and had experienced it from both sides, for a good number had probably worked for the Confederates.

The men of the United States Colored Troops

came from every restricted walk of black American life, and from every region where people of African descent resided. Several regiments had men who were born in Africa, Canada, or Chile. The Eighty-third United States Colored Infantry had two men who were from the Cherokee Nation.

As civilians they had worked at occupations which were open to black men. Those in the Massachusetts Fifty-fifth regiment, for example, were mostly farmers or laborers, but there were also barbers, waiters, cooks, blacksmiths, painters, teamsters, grooms, hostlers (people who took care of horses and mules), coachmen, coopers (who made and repaired barrels), and sailors. There was a machinist, rope-maker, fisherman, tinker (a person who fixed pots and pans), glass grinder, broom maker and one student. Out of the 980 men in the regiment, 247 had been held in slavery.

In Company K, Twenty-first United States Colored Infantry, in South Carolina, most of the men had been held in slavery; however, they had many of the same occupations as the enlisted men in the Fifty-fifth. The majority had been laborers or farmers; there were also blacksmiths, a boatman, butler, carpenter, cartmen, coachmen, cooper, driver, engineer, mail carrier, stockman, teamster, wagoner, and a waiter. The men in this company had been born in South Carolina, Virginia, Florida, Alabama, and New York.[14]

Other occupations represented in a sampling of companies were mason, riverman, shingler, cobbler, tailor, cigarmaker, tinsmith, sawyer (a person who saws timber), and iron worker. There were thirteen black chaplains and eight black surgeons in the United States Colored Troops. Thomas J. Morgan made the important point in his *Reminiscences of Services with Colored Troops* that there was the

The men of the United States
Colored Troops welcomed the chance
to fight for their own freedom.

same range of intelligence, physical ability, and aptitude for military life that would be found among the same number of white men.[15]

What made many of these soldiers different from their white counterparts is that they were fighting for their liberty and manhood and for better lives for their children. To them the challenge was given to prove slavery and racism wrong. They knew that if they failed, then the movement to enlist black men into the army would also be considered a failure.

VIII

CAMP LIFE

One more valiant soldier here,
One more valiant soldier here,
One more valiant soldier here,
To help me bear [the] cross.

Spiritual sung by the men in the
First South Carolina Volunteers

By January 1863, the men of the First South Carolina Volunteers were well on their way to being organized into a fine regiment. There were 740 men in training, and about 100 new recruits were expected from St. Augustine, Florida. The commander was Colonel Thomas W. Higginson, an abolitionist minister from Massachusetts who sincerely believed in the ability, talent, and intelligence of the men he led.

The camp was on the grounds of what had been a rich plantation on Hilton Head Island, South Carolina. The barns, dairy house, smokehouse, and other plantation buildings were falling apart. A few dogs, pigs, and chickens roamed through the rubble of the abandoned buildings. Children played outside the old slave cabins, while the women and elderly people remaining on the plantation tried to survive.

Some of the women worked as laundresses in the camp; others sold baskets and rugs they made from grass and palmetto fronds. Some of the old men found employment as servants to the officers in the camp. Those who were strong enough worked in the camp as laborers. The plantation that had been their prison became an instrument for their freedom.

The younger, stronger men were still on the plantation grounds also, but beyond the oak trees and the plantation buildings, where tufts of coarse grass grew out of the sandy soil and the long, sharp leaves of the palmetto trees seemed to reach for the sun. They were now soldiers and lived and worked in the camp.

Around the white army tents were the regimental hospital; cook houses for each company; a mess house made of palmetto fronds, where the men ate; and a guardhouse. The most popular structure was the large circular tent where classes were held.

The camp buzzed with excitement and activity during the day: The command of an officer to his men, "Shoulder arms!" The sound of marching feet as another group drilled, forming squares, the men moving in unison as if they were one body. Laughter rang out from a group of men at target practice—one fellow had fired his gun into the ground, instead of at the target.

In the evening, camp fires were built in small enclosures made from palmetto leaves. Some of the men held a shout—joyously clapping, dancing, and singing hymns. At another camp fire, the men listened to one of their fellow soldiers preach. "I have left my wife in the land of bondage; my little ones, they say every night, where is my father? But when I die, when the blessed morning rises, when I shall stand in the glory, with one foot on the water and one foot on the land, then, O Lord, I shall see my wife and my little children once more."[1] Some of the men sat praying quietly.

A few of the soldiers were cleaning their guns while others rehearsed what they'd learned at drill

Training was an important aspect of camp life.

practice. From some camp fires came chants of *cat, hat, pat,* as the men learned to read from a primer. And at yet another camp fire, the men in red pantaloons pranced about to the violin playing of one of the soldiers, as if they were at a square dance with their women, and sang, "Now-lead-the-lady over."

Colonel Higginson said that he found no vices among the men: "Since I took command I have heard of no man intoxicated, and there has been but one small quarrel. I suppose that scarcely a white regiment in the army shows so little swearing."[2]

The atmosphere of the First South Carolina camp was quite different from that of the Fifty-fourth Massachusetts in Readville, Massachusetts, where January and February are much colder. The first black recruits who reported to Readville found muddy fields and gray skies, with dull, large barracks to match.

In spite of the bleak environment, the camp was as lively as the First South Carolina camp. The men were cheerful and very interested in drilling. In a report about the regiment an officer wrote that the barracks, cook houses, and kitchens were clean and well run. He said that they were the best he had ever seen. He also noted that the men took pride in their appearance and in the way they cared for their arms and other military supplies. He added that "there was less drunkenness in this regiment than in any that had ever left Massachusetts. . . . no regiments were ever more . . . proper in their behavior than the Fifty-fourth and Fifty-fifth Massachusetts Colored Volunteers."[3]

Whether the camp was on a former Southern plantation or at a Northern military facility, and whether the regiment was a black one or a white one, the routines of drill and training and the rigors of army life were generally the same. However, there was one activity that marked the life in the camps of the black regiments—schooling.

For many of the men, especially those who had been in slavery, this was the first opportunity they'd ever had to attend school and many were eager to learn. In the South, teaching a slave to read and write was a crime, punishable by fines and imprisonment. In some parts of the South a slave could be punished for holding a pencil or walking with a book. And in the North, black children were, for the most part, barred from attending white schools.

"These recruits came to us ignorant of books," George R. Sherman, an officer, said of the men in the Seventh Regiment United States Colored Troops. Most of the men in his regiment had been slaves on plantations on the eastern shore of Maryland and Virginia. Only a few of the freeborn men could write their names. Sherman wrote that the men, in order to compensate for being unable to read or write, worked very hard to learn their military duties, and also took the opportunity to learn very seriously.

Classes were organized in each company for the non-commissioned officers [sergeants], and they would go out among the men to teach them the A, B, C; and except when military duty prevented, these classes were kept up almost to the day of discharge. It was an interesting sight, that might have been witnessed almost everyday during the first year, to see groups of five or six men gathered around a primer or spelling book, learning the alphabet, and as time passed on, to see those same men writing letters to their friends, or reading a book or paper.

When the regiment was disbanded, after a full three years' service, nearly all of them could read, a large percentage could write fairly well, and many had acquired considerable knowledge of the elementary branches [of knowledge], and, what was of even greater importance, all had learned self-reliance and self-respect and went back to their homes with views enlarged, ambition aroused, and their interest in the outside world thoroughly awakened.[4]

Thomas J. Morgan, colonel of the Fourteenth United States Colored Infantry, wrote that school was an important part of the black soldier's training. "In addition to ordinary instruction in the duties required of the soldier, we established in every company a regular school, teaching the men to read and write."[5]

Colonel Higginson of the First South Carolina Volunteers said that the men of his regiment never tired of the spelling book. "The Chaplain is getting up a schoolhouse, where he will soon teach them as regularly as he can."[6]

Susie King Taylor, a young black woman who had escaped to the Sea Islands with her family when the war broke out and Union soldiers took over the islands, was on St. Simon's Island teaching at a small school when she was asked to work at the First South Carolina camp as a laundress. She was also a nurse and a teacher. She wrote: "I taught a great many of the comrades in company E to read and write when they were off duty, nearly all were anxious to learn. My husband taught some also when it was convenient for him. . . . I gave my services willingly for four years and three months without receiving a dollar. I was glad, however, to be allowed to go with the regiment, to care for the sick and afflicted comrades."[7]

A captain of the Fourteenth Rhode Island Heavy Artillery wrote: "During this period, we organized schools for the instruction of our men. While some of them were comparatively well educated and were very serviceable in various kinds of clerical work, a large proportion were destitute of the most rudimentary knowledge."[8]

Many of the white troops, too, could barely read or write. Records indicate that for forty years before the Civil War, possibly between one-third and one-fourth of all soldiers could not sign their names.[9]

Susie King Taylor taught the soldiers at the camp of the
First South Carolina Volunteers to read and write.

However, as Colonel Higginson wrote, "The alphabet must always be a very incidental business in a camp." If the soldiers are not drilled and well disciplined, they may behave like the Union soldiers at Bull Run who fled the battle in panic. Preparing the men as quickly as possible to be able to fight was the first order of business in the regiments. As the companies that made up a regiment were formed, drilling and discipline were the most important aspects of their training. Drilling began at once, along with the often grueling fatigue duty, consisting of cleaning, digging ditches, building shelters, hauling equipment, and more.

The soldiers in the USCT had to dive into battle immediately. They did not have many months of training as did the white troops who had enlisted earlier. The soldiers of the Fifty-fourth Massachusetts, for example, were recruited in February 1863, and by that July participated in a major battle.

During drill the men had to learn various military commands that they would need in combat. They also had to be able to understand and execute commands quickly. On the battlefield, not following an order immediately could mean injury or death. Colonel Thomas Morgan said that "The six companies at Bridgeport [Alabama] were kept very busily at work, and had but little opportunity for drill. Notwithstanding these difficulties, however, considerable progress was made in both drill and discipline."[10]

Colonel Higginson, along with many of the other officers who left regimental histories and memoirs, said that the black soldiers were excellent at drill and superior to most of the white regiments. He stated, "The adaptedness of the freed slaves for drill and discipline is now thoroughly demonstrated, and must soon be universally acknowledged."[11]

An officer of the Third United States Colored Cavalry stated that "It is worthy of note that this regiment was enlisted, organized and drilled in the field. Always on the picket [guard] lines, never exempt from attack, and always within range of the enemies' guns, frequently leaving the drill ground to repel an attack."[12]

Not all officers were like Higginson and Morgan, who had high expectations for the men they commanded. Officers who treated their recruits like children and who believed that the men could not be good soldiers did not have successful organizations. Officers who looked beyond the color of the men's skin and saw real people were able to develop excellent companies and regiments. Thomas Morgan examined the mental as well as the physical state of the men he recruited. "I plied them with questions as to their history, their experience with the army, their motives for becoming soldiers, their ideas of army life, their hopes for the future. . . . The result of this careful examination convinced me that these men, though black in skin, had men's hearts, and only needed right handling to develop into magnificent soldiers."[13]

Some officers trained certain enlisted men to perform clerical and managerial duties, the same kind of work that non-commissioned officers in white units did. The officers taught them army rules, military tactics, and reading and writing—freeing the officers from piles of paperwork such as preparing muster rolls, lists of clothing and equipment. The officers were then free to spend more time training the men.

Many officers were pleased with the progress of their troops. However, the racial attitudes of the times still affected the way people of African descent were perceived. Discipline was harsh. One observer

wrote that officers meted out harsh and painful pun-
ishments for minor offenses. They would "buck and
gag" soldiers—keep them tied up for hours in a
crouching position, or hang them from their thumbs
for long periods with only their feet able to touch the
ground.[14]

It is obvious that black troops were no worse than
their white counterparts. Like white draftees, they
came into the army as civilians, ignorant of military
life. However, many of the fugitives from the Confederate army camps were not as inexperienced about
the military as the "raw recruits," white and black,
from the North. They had already experienced military life in the Confederate camps. They had also
survived the horrors and hardships of slavery and
were used to deprivation. They were strong, tough
men able to deal with army life.

But, as the men of the USCT prepared themselves to become soldiers, they found that they still
had to face prejudice and racism from the people
they were fighting for as well as from the people
they were fighting against. The USCT had many
detractors who did not believe that any good would
result from allowing black men to join the army.

IX

THE OTHER ENEMY

Three cheers for Massachusetts and seven dollars a month!

Battle-Cry of the Fifty-fourth Regiment

The women worked in the fields under a scorching Louisiana sun as they'd always done. Life was even more difficult now, however, since many of the men had gone off to fight with the Yankees and the women were left on the plantation, along with the children and the old mothers and fathers. They were terrified of the overseer who made sure that they did their work, and the master of the plantation, who yelled at them and beat them for the slightest offense.

Someone from the plantation, though, had managed to get a message over to a nearby Union army camp where many of the men from the plantation were in the USCT. The women wondered how long they'd be able to stand the beatings and the extra hours of work heaped on them because the men were gone.

When they thought that they could not work another minute or take another beating, fortunately, the men returned. Dressed in their Union blues, and carrying their muskets, they entered the plantation and removed their families to settlements organized for fugitives.

Families left on Southern plantations were a constant source of worry for the black soldier from the South. Sometimes his family would be sold when a man left to join the Union army, or the family members still on the plantation would be abused by the plantation owner. Not all of the men in the USCT who had families on Southern plantations could save them as the Louisiana soldiers did. Concern for wives, parents, and children still held in slavery was one of the many pressures inflicted on the black Civil War soldiers by their other enemy—racism.

The black soldiers seemed to be fighting a different war than that of other soldiers from either the North or the South. Although finally accepted into the army, their status as soldiers or "real Yankees," as one Confederate officer stated, was constantly questioned. They had to prove themselves over and over again. Once Northern resistance to accepting black soldiers in the army had been broken, the next battle was with the military and government officials who tried to limit the soldiers' roles. In some white regiments there was resentment that some black soldiers had positions that were equal to those that were held by white soldiers.

Colonel Robert Cowden, who recruited men for the First West Tennessee Infantry of African Descent (later named the Fifty-ninth Regiment of United States Colored Infantry), said that as he organized the regiment, he selected the brightest and most capable black men to fill vacant first-sergeant positions. The white men who were first sergeants in the regiment could not stand to have blacks on an equal footing with them, so they asked to be discharged from the regiment.

At times racism led to ridiculous actions. Once, when an officer took a group of new black recruits on a march, a group of white Union soldiers posing as Confederates fired on them to see whether the black troops would run or fire back. They did not run but, much to the surprise of the white soldiers, fired back and sent them scampering off.

At other times racism led to mindlessly cruel behavior. Men in an Illinois regiment stationed in Mississippi asked a fugitive who might have been working in the camp to dance for them. As the man danced on a box, the soldiers set off gunpowder under the box and blew the man twenty feet into the air.[1]

In her journals, Charlotte Forten wrote about her impression of an army officer. "Capt. T. is a perfect little popinjay, and he and a Colonel somebody who didn't look any too sensible, talked in a very smart manner, evidently for our especial benefit. The word 'nigger' was plentifully used. . . . But if they are a fair example of army officers, I [should] pray to see as little of them as possible."[2]

Many people, after accepting the fact that black men would be in the military, felt that they should be limited to garrison (guarding a fort or area already captured) and fatigue duty. Even the language of the Emancipation Proclamation implied that performing fatigue and garrison duty would be the main functions of the black soldiers: "And I further declare and make known that such persons, of suitable condition, will be received into the armed service, to garrison forts, positions, stations and other places, and to man vessels of all sorts in said service."

As late as 1864, after black regiments had proven themselves in battle, a soldier in Brownsville, Texas, wrote in his diary:

Many people—both in the military and in civilian life—
wanted to keep blacks relegated to menial roles.

> I have previous to this Spoken of the Corps d'Afrique. . . . They are the laborers of the Army—Upon our arrival . . . there were dozens of heavily loaded vessels. The work of unloading these boats was performed by [Negroes]—nor was this all—bridges were to be made, troops to be ferried, roads to [be] made—in fact there was daily labor for hundreds of men and which of necessity must have been performed by soldiers had not we had [Negroes] with us.
>
> At this place forts and fortifications were to be made requiring the labor of hundreds of men for months.
>
> Streets were to be swept and cleaned daily and this is work of a very disagreeable character and for one I thank the originators of the Corps d'Afrique for taking from us such labor as belong to menials.
>
> Today their whole force is at work and hour after hour through the long hours under the heat of a scorching sun they labor and bring their works of labor to perfection. They are a fine looking set of men—all fair specimens of their native Africa. And while our soldiers pride themselves on the nice condition of their arms, the Corps d'Afrique are proud of the fine conditions of their picks and spaids [spades].[3]

Some white soldiers never changed their attitudes toward their black comrades, even as the war neared its end. A soldier wrote in his diary on January 18, 1865, "We have seen several Negro regiments here. They make pretty good looking soldiers but our boys don't think much of them. They still say this is a white man's war."[4]

Colonel Fox of the Fifty-fifth Massachusetts wrote in his record of the regiment that it had to perform excessive fatigue duty which destroyed drill and discipline. However, he added, the men kept up their military bearing in spite of the fact that many people felt it was more appropriate for blacks to carry shovels rather than muskets.

Thomas Wentworth Higginson said that he

would not command black troops if they were to be used only for garrison and fatigue duty. "It would be intolerable to go out to South Carolina and find myself, after all, at the head of a mere plantation guard or a day-school in uniform."[5] Thomas J. Morgan, colonel of the Fourteenth United States Colored Infantry, wrote, "I made earnest efforts to get the regiment united and relieved from so much labor, in order that they might be prepared for efficient field services as soldiers."[6]

Captain Luis Emilio described the grueling fatigue duty that the Massachusetts Fifty-forth had to perform during the siege of Fort Wagner in 1863. "Eighteen bomb or splinter proof service-magazines made, as well as eighty-nine emplacements for guns ... Forty-six thousand sand-bags had been filled, hundreds of gabions [cylinders filled with earth] and fascines [bundles of sticks used to line trenches] made, and wharves and landings constructed. Of the nineteen thousand days' work performed by infantry, the colored troops had done one half, though numerically they were to white troops as one to ten."[7]

The white officers in the USCT were ridiculed and stigmatized because they led black troops. "At the time that the work of organizing colored troops began in the West," Emilio wrote, "there was a great deal of bitter prejudice against the movement. White troops threatened to desert if the plan should be really carried out. Those who entered the service were stigmatized as 'nigger officers,' and [N]egro soldiers were hooted at and mistreated by white troops."[8] Captain Emilio also reported that, "Lieut. John S. Marcy, Fifty-second Pennsylvania, when directed to join the Fifth-fourth detail for duty ... refused to do so, saying, 'I will not do duty with colored troops.' He was arrested and court-martialled, and, by General Foster's order, dishonorably dismissed."[9]

Captain Luis F. Emilio
Massachusetts
Fifty-fourth Regiment

Some of the officers viewed their troops as children and not men. Though Colonel Higginson was sincerely committed to abolition and the black soldier, he too could be condescending—not really understanding the men and seeing them through eyes clouded by the stereotypes of the time.

The demeanor of my men to each other is very courteous, and yet I see none of that sort of upstart conceit which is sometimes offensive among free [N]egroes at the North, the dandy-barber strut. This is an agreeable surprise, for I feared that freedom and regimentals would produce precisely that.

 They seem the world's perpetual children, docile, gay, and lovable, in the midst of this war for freedom on which they have intelligently entered.[10]

One of the hardest battles the black soldier fought was to get the same pay as the white soldiers. Black soldiers were fighting for their freedom and self-respect, but for a long period served without pay. They were recruited with the understanding that their pay would be the same as white soldiers'— $13.00 per month. The first pay in 1863 received by the Thirty-third United States Colored Infantry and the Louisiana Native Guards was $13.00 for privates and $21.00 for sergeants.

However, on June 4, 1863, the War Department changed its policy. It stated that the Militia Act of July 17, 1862, indicated that the black men enlisted for military service would be paid $10.00 per month—$3.00 of this for clothing—the same rate as paid laborers hired by the government.

The soldiers refused to accept the unequal pay. Isaac Hill wrote in his sketch of his Connecticut regiment:

> I passed up the line of tents, and saw the Major in a wagon—he informed me that the Paymaster had arrived. When I made this known to the 29th Regiment the boys were much pleased, for they had not received any money since their enlistment, but soon their spirits fell when they learned they would receive only $7 per month. . . . After the companies all expressed their indignation at the small sum of $7 per month, the officers called them in line and told them they would receive $16 the next pay day, and they had better take this—at the same time promising them that in the future they should receive full pay. They did as he wished. This has been the failing with the colored race—they are always ready to comply with wrong teachings of strange gods, especially when they come from white men, and that is the reason we cannot be a united nation. I would not and did not accept of the $7 per month, and I stood entirely alone. All in my company took that sum but myself.

Hill went on to say that he would fight and die for his country without wages if the government could not afford to give him soldier's pay. Hill also worried about his family. "When I consider the sacrifice I have made of my beloved family, and think that the general government does nothing for them, and then to insult me with the sum of $7 per month. . . ."[11]

All of the men of the Fifth-fourth Massachusetts refused to accept the reduced pay when the paymaster arrived in camp on September 27, 1863. The regiment had already fought in the battle of Fort Wagner where it suffered great losses. The men who died in that battle were never paid.

The men and their families suffered when the soldiers were not paid. Often families in the North had to depend solely on the husband's wages for survival. Some states and cities had organizations to help soldiers' families who needed money, but the families of black soldiers would be turned away when they applied for temporary aid. The wife and children of Sergeant Stephen A. Swails of the Fifty-fourth Massachusetts ended up in a poorhouse because he had no money to send them.

The chaplain of the regiment was also denied equal pay. "Samuel Harrison, Chaplain of the Fifty-fourth Regiment Massachusetts Volunteers (colored troops)," wrote the army paymaster, "asks pay at the usual rate of chaplains,—one hundred dollars per month and two rations, which, he being of African descent, I decline paying, under Act of Congress, July 17, 1862. . . . The chaplain declines receiving any thing less. . . ."[12]

Sergeant William Walker of the Twenty-first United States Colored Infantry paid the ultimate price when he demanded fair treatment. He was convicted and executed for mutiny when he refused to work because he had not received the pay that he had been promised. Charges of mutiny were more prevalent in USCT than in white units, and the punishment for minor offenses were often severe.[13]

Governor Andrew of Massachusetts said of Walker's execution, "The Government which found no law to pay him except as a nondescript and a contraband, nevertheless found law enough to shoot him as a soldier."[14]

The men of the First South Carolina, Higginson's Regiment, also refused to accept reduced pay. Susie King Taylor, the nurse and teacher for the regiment, wrote:

> The first colored troops did not receive any pay for eighteen months. . . . The men had to depend wholly on what they received from the commissary, established by General Saxton. A great many of these men had large families, and as they had no money to give them, their wives were obliged to support themselves and children by washing for the officers of the gunboats and the soldiers, and making cakes and pies which they sold to the boys in camp. Finally, in 1863 the government decided to give them half pay, but the men would not accept this. They wanted 'full pay' or nothing. They preferred rather to give their services to the state, which they did until 1864, when the government granted them full pay, with all the back pay due.[15]

In some regiments, the officers refused to accept their pay, too, until their men received fair wages. Pressure against the government policy mounted. United States Attorney General Edward Bates said that the government had agreed to pay black soldiers the same as whites and that it was now breaking the terms of its own agreement.

According to the law, if the agreement with the black units was broken, these units could be mustered out of the service. The military needed the manpower provided by black troops, and in June 1864, equal pay for all soldiers was provided, dating from January 1, 1864. Back pay at the same rate as white soldiers was to be offered only to black soldiers who had been free on April 19, 1861. The soldiers had to take an oath stating that they were free.

The men of the Fifty-fourth took the oath, each swearing that he "owed no man unrequited labor on or before the 19th day of April, 1861." The regiment called this their "Quaker Oath." Even the men who had been held in slavery at that time took the oath, because, they said by "God's higher law," they were free men.[16]

The black troops continued to protest, demanding that men who had been held in slavery also receive equal pay. It was not until 1865, the year the war ended, that Congress passed a law providing equal pay for all black soldiers.

Another obstacle that the USCT had to overcome was the government's policy of having only white officers. John F. Shorter of the Fifty-fifth Massachusetts was commissioned as a second lieutenant by Governor John Andrew, but the War Department refused to muster him in as an officer. Two other men in the regiment were also refused commissions, which upset the enlisted men. The USCT men then had no opportunity to advance in rank. Colonel Higginson said that Color-Sergeant Rivers deserved to be commissioned as an officer, but knew that it would not be accepted. "I should have tried to obtain commissions for him and several others before I left the regiment," he wrote.[17] His successor, Colonel Trowbridge, tried to get commissions for Rivers and another soldier, but the War Department refused.

General Benjamin Butler made Milton Holland

After the Enrollment Act, black soldiers
finally received full pay.

a captain right on the battlefield in Virginia, where he was wounded in 1864. The War Department refused to grant the commission, however, because Holland was of African descent. In spite of this government policy, eventually about one hundred men of African descent earned commissions as officers.[18]

The Massachusetts Fifty-fourth had four black officers: Chaplain Samuel Harrison, Lieutenant Stephen A. Swails, Lieutenant Frank M. Welch, and Lieutenant Peter Vogelsang.

The Louisiana Native Guards always had their own black officers. However, when General Nathaniel P. Banks took over the command of the Department of the Gulf, he tried to replace the black officers of these regiments with white ones as vacancies occurred. A soldier who had been in the Second Louisiana Native Guards and then transferred to the Fifty-fourth Massachusetts said that recruiting suffered in the area because Banks replaced black officers with white ones.

William Wells Brown described the disappointment of the soldiers when their officers were taken away: "The colored soldiers were deeply pained at seeing the officers of their own color and choice taken from them; for they were much attached to their commanders, some of whom were special favorites with the whole regiment. Among these were First Lieut. Joseph Howard of Company I, and Second Lieut. Joseph G. Parker, of Company C."[19]

Discrimination also resulted in improper health precautions and poor medical care for the black soldiers. Proportionately more soldiers in black regiments died from illness than men in white units. One reason for the high mortality rate was that military authorities believed black men could withstand all tropical diseases; therefore, many black regiments were assigned to unhealthy areas where the men and their officers fell ill from typhoid fever, cholera, dysentery, malaria, and pneumonia.

Nearly 800 men died of disease in one black regiment and another regiment had 524 deaths in less than a year. Regimental hospitals (medicare facilities in the camp) gave all their troops adequate care; however, general hospitals on army posts had separate and unequal facilities for black and white troops. The facilities for seriously ill black soldiers were substandard, leading to higher death rates among black hospitalized soldiers. The hospital for the Corps d'Afrique in New Orleans, for example, was described as dirty, with no regular routine or discipline.[20]

Black soldiers suffered poor medical care also because of the lack of qualified doctors. Only eight black surgeons received commissions in the USCT, and it was difficult to get white surgeons to accept assignments in black regiments. One of the black doctors in the USCT was Alexander Augusta, who had been trained at Trinity College in Toronto, Canada, where he became a prominent physician. He accepted a commission in the USCT and was assigned to Camp Stanton in Maryland, where he was the head surgeon. The white assistant surgeons wrote to President Lincoln requesting Dr. Augusta's removal because they did not want to work under a black doctor. Dr. Augusta was removed from Camp Stanton.

Dr. Augusta suffered another humiliating experience when he was attacked on a train while on his way from Baltimore to Philadelphia. Two men tore the officer's insignia from the doctor's uniform, while a mob watched. He also had to fight for a surgeon's pay. Like the enlisted men, his salary was only $7.00

a month. He waited fifty-three weeks before he was paid according to his rank of major.[21]

The men and officers of the USCT faced another danger. The Confederate congress passed an act stating that neither the black soldiers nor their white officers would be treated as prisoners of war if captured. The officers would be executed and the troops sold into slavery. Frederick Douglass and other black leaders were outraged. In the past, Douglass had counseled black men to join the army even though they would not be granted equal rights. Justice and fair treatment would come later, he said. The immediate goal was to end slavery.

However, when the Confederate congress declared that they would execute and enslave USCT officers and soldiers, Douglass refused to continue recruiting black enlistees unless the government did something to protect the men in the USCT, and gave the black troops the same pay and opportunity for advancement available to white soldiers. Abraham Lincoln issued a counterorder threatening to execute a Southern soldier for every Union soldier killed in violation of the rules of war and put every captured Southern soldier to hard labor if the Confederates executed USCT officers and enslaved black troops. Douglass resumed recruiting, while continuing to press the government for fair treatment of soldiers of African descent.

How prisoners were treated depended on which Confederates captured them. In some instances, Southerners carried out their threat to execute prisoners. Fort Pillow in Tennessee was garrisoned by a large number of black troops. On April 14, 1864, it was attacked by Confederate forces. The Union soldiers surrendered the fort after a battle, but many black soldiers were then killed by the attackers.

TO COLORED MEN!

FREEDOM,

Protection, Pay, and a Call to Military Duty!

On the 1st day of January, 1863, the President of the United States proclaimed FREE-
DOM to over THREE MILLIONS OF SLAVES. This decree is to be enforced by all the power of
the Nation. On the 21st of July last he issued the following order:

PROTECTION OF COLORED TROOPS.

"WAR DEPARTMENT, ADJUTANT GENERAL'S OFFICE, }
WASHINGTON, July 21. }

"*General Order,* No. 233.

"The following order of the President is published for the information and government of all concerned:—

EXECUTIVE MANSION, WASHINGTON, July 30.

'"It is the duty of every Government to give protection to its citizens, of whatever class, color, or condition, and especially to
those who are duly organized as soldiers in the public service. The law of nations, and the usages and customs of war, as carried on
by civilized powers, permit no distinction as to color in the treatment of prisoners of war as public enemies. To sell or enslave any
captured person on account of his color, is a relapse into barbarism, and a crime against the civilization of the age.
'"The Government of the United States will give the same protection to all its soldiers, and if the enemy shall sell or enslave any
one because of his color, the offense shall be punished by retaliation upon the enemy's prisoners in our possession. It is, therefore
ordered, for every soldier of the United States, killed in violation of the laws of war, a rebel soldier shall be executed; and for every
one enslaved by the enemy, or sold into slavery, a rebel soldier shall be placed at hard labor on the public works, and continued at such
labor until the other shall be released and receive the treatment due to prisoners of war.
'"ABRAHAM LINCOLN."'

'"By order of the Secretary of War.
'"E. D. TOWNSEND, Assistant Adjutant General."'

That the President is in earnest the rebels soon began to find out, as witness the following order from his Secretary of War:

"WAR DEPARTMENT, WASHINGTON CITY, August 8, 1863.

"SIR: Your letter of the 3d inst., calling the attention of this Department to the cases of Orin H. Brown, William H. Johnston,
and Wm. Wilson, three colored men captured on the gunboat Isaac Smith, has received consideration. This Department has directed
that three rebel prisoners of South Carolina, if there be any such in our possession, and if not, three others, be confined in close custody
and held as hostages for Brown, Johnston and Wilson, and that the fact be communicated to the rebel authorities at Richmond.
"Very respectfully your obedient servant,
"EDWIN M. STANTON, Secretary of War.

"The Hon. GIDEON WELLES, Secretary of the Navy."

And retaliation will be our practice now—man for man—to the bitter end.

LETTER OF CHARLES SUMNER,

Written with reference to the Convention held at Poughkeepsie, July 15th and 16th, 1863, to promote Colored Enlistments.

BOSTON, July 13th, 1863.

"I doubt if, in times past, our country could have expected from colored men any patriotic service. Such service is the return for
protection. But now that protection has begun, the service should begin also. Nor should relative rights and duties be weighed with
nicety. It is enough that our country, aroused at last to a sense of justice, seeks to enrol colored men among its defenders.
"If my counsels should reach such persons, I would say: enlist at once. Now is the day and now is the hour. Help to overcome
your cruel enemies now battling against your country, and in this way you will surely overcome those other enemies hardly less cruel,
here at home, who will still seek to degrade you. This is not the time to hesitate or to higgle. Do your duty to our country, and you
will set an example of generous self-sacrifice which will conquer prejudice and open all hearts.
"Very faithfully yours,
"CHARLES SUMNER."

The men defeated at the siege of Port Hudson were also treated harshly. William Wells Brown wrote that "Humanity should not forget, that, at the surrender of Port Hudson, not a single colored man could be found alive, although thirty-five were known to have been taken prisoner during the siege. All had been murdered."[22] In contrast, soldiers in the Fifty-fourth Massachusetts who were captured on James Island and at Fort Wagner were imprisoned.

After the war the government conducted an inquiry on the treatment of prisoners. A former inmate at Andersonville, one of the worst prisons for captured Union soldiers, said: "No medicine was given to colored soldiers, although they were sick with the scurvy and other diseases, and applied to the surgeon for them. I saw them take one of the colored soldiers and strip him, and give him thirty lashes until the blood ran, and his back was all cut up. This was because he was not able to go out and work. . . ."[23]

Whether fugitives or well-educated professionals like Dr. Augusta, the soldiers of the USCT had to continually battle the second enemy—racism. They were determined to win that battle also.

After angry demands from black leaders, the president took steps to protect the men of the USCT.

X

SOLDIER'S WORK

When I told another one who wanted to "fight for freedom," that he might lose his life, he replied: "But my people will be free."

Col. Thomas J. Morgan

It is prowess on the battlefield that earns men respect in war, and the men in the USCT knew this. Until each man had a chance to participate in major military engagements, his worth as a soldier remained in doubt. Would the black man fight? Many Americans held to their idea of blacks as cowards, and said no, he would not stand up and fight like a man. The black soldiers knew that they had to prove that idea wrong. The men of two black Louisiana regiments were among the first black troops to offer proof.

The First Louisiana Native Guards, formerly the Native Guards, were educated free men of African descent. Many owned property and businesses. Their regimental officers were black. In contrast, the men of the Third Louisiana Native Guards had been held in slavery for most of their lives and were called "contraband" by their white officers. On the morning of May 27, 1863, the two regiments went into battle.

It was a hot, dry morning in Port Hudson, Louisiana. Captain André Callioux, Lieutenant John Crowder, and the rest of the men in the First and Third Louisiana regiments waited along with white regiments for the battle to begin. The black regiments were part of a large Union force trying to gain control of Port Hudson on the Mississippi River.[1]

The blue line of federal troops under the leadership of General Banks waited for the order to charge. "The weatherwise watched the red masses of the morning, and still hoped for a shower to cool the air, and lay the dust, before the work of death commenced. . . . The very atmosphere seemed as if it were from an overheated oven."[2]

The men began to put aside all unnecessary articles—sacks, blankets, and other personal items. "Capt. Callioux walked proudly up and down the line, and smilingly greeted the familiar faces of his company. Officers and privates of the white regiments looked on as they saw these men at the front, and asked each other what they thought would be the result. Would these blacks stand fire? Was not the test by which they were to be tried too severe?"[3]

William Wells Brown wrote about the experiences of black soldiers in the Civil War.

The Union commanders thought that this would be an easy victory. When the Union forces had come into the area several days earlier, they'd taken the Confederates by surprise. The Southerners had set up strong defenses to the south and east of Port Hudson, expecting an attack from those directions. But the federals had approached Port Hudson from the north. The Southerners had to put up more defenses quickly.

Their battery of guns situated on a steep slope was hidden behind a natural barrier of fallen trees, shrubs, and bushes. A swamp lay on one side of the road and the steep hill rose on the other side. A Confederate engineer had diverted water from the Mississippi in order to flood the road to the hill.

At last the order to charge cut the hot air and part of the blue line moved. Troops on one flank of the black regiments charged first, but could not penetrate the strong defenses—both natural and constructed—thrown up by the rebels.

Around 10 A.M. the black regiments were called. As they marched across a bridge and toward the enemy's cannon and other artillery that were trained down on them from the slope, riflemen hidden in the hills began to fire. They pushed forward, even as some of their force dropped among them. Using fallen logs and trees as a shield, they left the woods and came to within 600 yards (549m) of the Confederates. There they formed two battle lines. The First Louisiana Native Guards led the charge to the Confederate lines, followed by the Third. The blue line of black troops was thinned, but the men kept coming, closing the gaps left by the dead and wounded.

In the middle of the battle, two black former officers, First Lieutenant Joseph Howard of Company I, and Second Lieutenant Joseph G. Parker of Company C, returned to the regiment. They had been forced to give up their commissions because General Banks refused to have black officers. When Howard and Parker found out that their old regiment was participating in this major assault, they volunteered to come back as privates. However, "Instead of being placed as privates in the ranks, they were both immediately assigned to the command of a company . . . from sheer necessity, because the white officers of these companies, feeling that the colored soldiers were put in the front of the battle owing to their complexion, were not willing to risk their lives, and had thrown up [given up] their commissions."[4]

As the battle raged, "shells from the rebel guns cut down trees three feet [.91m] in diameter, and they fell, at one time burying a whole company beneath their branches."[5] Throughout the battle, Captain Callioux led his company. A rifle ball had broken his arm above the elbow and even as it dangled at his side, in his other hand he "held his unsheathed sword gleaming in the rays of the sun; and his hoarse, faint voice was heard cheering on his men."[6] At about one o'clock, when the last charge was made, Callioux was struck down and killed. Lieutenant John H. Crowder was also killed in the Port Hudson battle, along with approximately two hundred other men. The Union suffered a resounding loss, due in part to poor planning by the commanders.

Each time the black regiments charged they were mowed down by the Confederate batteries until finally they were ordered to retreat by the commanders in the field. The black regiments lost about 20 percent of their men.[7] They had proven that blacks could stand up to bullets as well as whites did. They neither ran nor hid, but made attempt after futile attempt to penetrate the Confederate lines.

Witnesses praised the troops. An officer in the Third Louisiana Native Guards said that as his

troops were mostly contrabands, he had had some
fears about how they would perform. After the battle
he had no more doubts. They fought bravely and
even had to be held back so that they did not go too
far without support.[8]

The Union would not gain control of Port Hudson
until July 8, 1863, when the Southerners surrendered it after the fall of Vicksburg. And it wasn't until
the surrender that the body of Callioux and the dead
black soldiers were removed from the battlefield. The
Confederates would not honor the cease-fire that allowed opposing armies to collect their casualties in
that section of the field where the black troops had
fought and fallen.

Twelve days after Port Hudson another group
of black soldiers was involved in a battle along the
Mississippi at Milliken's Bend. The Confederates
were trying to stop Union encroachments in the area.
The Union commander, Brigadier General Elias
Dennis, called up units from the Tenth Illinois Cavalry and the Ninth Louisiana (Colored) Infantry. Included in the units were newly recruited black
soldiers who were mostly freedmen from Mississippi
plantations. The troops were ordered to leave their
camp at Milliken's Bend to try to discover enemy
movements.

The men in the Illinois cavalry were angry at
having to serve with black troops who—to make the
situation worse—were new recruits. Perhaps they
had not heard about Port Hudson, for they predicted
that the new recruits would run at the first shot.

The black troops—armed with old Belgian rifles
and having only a few days' training—led the scout-
ing party and fought off a group of Confederate cavalry. No one was hurt in that skirmish. The colonel
leading them, however, saw a larger force of Confederate cavalry approaching. The colonel ordered his
men to retreat and the Confederates chased them.

The Illinois Cavalry, certain that the black soldiers were fleeing in panic, and needed help, galloped to the rescue, but they were routed by the Southerners. The black soldiers halted their retreat and turned to fire at the Confederates, thus helping the Illinois Cavalry to escape from the rebels.

The colonel and his men reached their camp safely and he then immediately sent for help, for he knew the Confederates would pursue them, and they did. In the early-morning hours of June 7, 1863, a Confederate brigade of about fifteen hundred men attacked the Union force of about one thousand men at Milliken's Bend.

The Union troops fought desperately, trying to fend off the Southern force. Hand-to-hand combat ensued, and the Confederates finally overran a portion of the riverbank and sprayed the entire line of troops with fire. Some of the soldiers from the Twenty-third Iowa ran as soon as the Confederates charged.[9] The black soldiers fought until they were forced to retreat to the riverbank, where for several hours they kept the Confederates from climbing the bank. Once Union gunboats joined the fight the Confederates retreated.

Those who had witnessed the battle had only praise for these inexperienced black troops. All fought well, except for one black regiment. Some of its troops did not act superbly in the battle when they couldn't see their officers. They thought they had been deserted.[10] An officer in one regiment said that he never wanted to hear anyone say again that blacks would not fight.[11]

But even the battles at Port Hudson and Milliken's Bend were not enough to convince everyone, and another black regiment in another theater of war once again took up the burden of proving the black man equal to other men.

XI

CAN I GET A WITNESS?

The old flag never touched the ground boys.

SERGEANT WILLIAM H. CARNEY
Fifty-fourth Massachusetts

On May 28, 1863, a day after the battle at Port Hudson, William Carney, Peter Vogelsang, Lewis Douglass, Samuel Sufshay, Stephen Swails, and the other men of the Fifty-fourth Regiment of Massachusetts Volunteer Infantry boarded the steamer *De Molay* in Boston Harbor and set sail for Hilton Head, South Carolina. They were to report to General David Hunter, who was finally seeing his dream of having black soldiers in the fight against Southern slavery become a reality.[1]

By June 4, the men were performing fatigue duty in the field. Robert Gould Shaw, the young colonel who led the regiment, was confident that his men were fine soldiers and was determined that they be given a chance to prove themselves. After spending a month on the Sea Islands, he wrote to his commanding officer, General Strong, voicing his fear that his regiment would not be allowed to participate in upcoming military operations.

St. Helena Island, July 6, 1863

Brig.-Gen. George C. Strong,

"I desire . . . to express to you my regret that my regiment no longer forms a part of the force under your command. I was the more disappointed at being left behind, that I had been given to understand that we were to have our share in the work in this department. I feel convinced too that my men are capable of better service than mere guerilla warfare, and I hoped to remain permanently under your command.

It seems to me quite important that the colored soldiers should be associated as much as possible with the white troops, in order that they may have other witnesses besides their own officers to what they are capable of doing. I trust that the present arrangement is not permanent."[2]

On July 8, the regiment was ordered to depart to James Island. From July 11 to July 16, the Fifty-fourth performed picket (guard) duty. On the morning of July 16, there was firing on the picket line. The Fifty-fourth was ordered to form a battle line as "fall in, fall in resounded on all sides, while drums of the several regiments were beating the long roll."[3]

Colonel Shaw marched the Fifty-fourth to the battle line and soon six companies of Confederate troops were marching toward them. "It seemed to Sergt. Vogelsang of Company H, who had his post at a palmetto-tree, that in a moment one hundred Rebels were swarming about him. . . ."[4] The Fifty-fourth helped the Tenth Connecticut, a white regiment, retreat from a position that meant certain destruction. When the Confederates came to within 600 yards (549m) of the Union line and opened fire, the Fifty-fourth regiment had its first fight."

They did not run, but returned the fire. "Not a man was out of place as the officers could see while they stood in rear of the lines, observing their men." General Terry, who commanded the operation on James Island, sent Shaw a message: "I am exceedingly pleased with the conduct of your regiment. They have done all they could do."[5] The island was evacuated that evening and after a grueling night march, through pouring rain over slippery bridges made of piling, they reached their destination—Cole's Island.

The men arrived at 5 A.M. on July 17 without food or rations, and that night at 10 P.M. they were on the move again, leaving for the trip to Morris Island. They arrived at Pawnee Landing at 9 A.M., and passed the camps of some white regiments. Word that the troops had helped the Tenth Connecticut had already reached these regiments and the Fifty-fourth received a warm greeting from the white soldiers. "Hurrah, boys," they exclaimed. "You saved the Tenth Connecticut."[6] Tired and hungry, they still had six more miles (about 9.6 km) to march before resting while they waited for transportation to Morris Island. They arrived on the island at 5 P.M. and Colonel Shaw reported to General Strong.

Before the regiment had landed, Union batteries had been shelling Fort Wagner, "throwing showers of sand from the slopes of Wagner into the air."[7] The fort was the main obstacle in the Union efforts to capture Fort Sumter and gain the city of Charleston. Fort Wagner sat on the northern end of Morris Island with the Atlantic Ocean on its eastern side. When the tide was in, the ocean waves lapped its walls. A creek lay on the western side of the fort. At high tide, only a narrow strip of land led to the fort. The federals shelled the fort in preparation for a major attack that evening. Captain Luis F. Emilio of the Fifty-fourth, Company C, described the island: "A fresh breeze blew that day; at times the sky was clear; the atmosphere lightened by recent rains, resounded with the thunders of an almost incessant cannonade. Smoke-clouds hung over the naval vessels, our batteries and those of the enemy."[8]

When Colonel Shaw reported, General Strong told him that his troops would storm Fort Wagner that night. Knowing that Shaw wanted his men to fight beside white troops, the general said, "You may lead the column. . . . Your men, I know, are worn out, but do as you choose."[9]

This moment was what Shaw had been waiting for—a chance for his regiment to prove themselves to their fellow soldiers and the rest of the doubting public. The regiment marched to Strong's headquarters, stopping at six o'clock for five minutes. The general saw how weary and hungry the men were. They had had no rations for two days. They'd been marching and traveling for hours. Although the general sympathized with them and wanted them to have food and drink, there was no time.

The regiment was sent immediately to the front. Shaw joined them a half hour later, after dining with General Strong. Because of the men who had been killed and wounded on James Island, the men who had to remain in camp as guards, and those on fatigue detail, there were only six hundred men from the Fifty-fourth on Morris Island that evening, along with fourteen other units formed into brigades.

General Strong addressed the men of the Fifty-fourth, encouraging them to fight for the honor of the state of Massachusetts and, once again, apologized for sending them into the battle tired and hungry. "Don't fire a musket on the way up," he warned them, "but go in and bayonet them at their guns." He looked in the direction of the color guard and said, "If this man should fall, who will lift the flag and carry it on?" Colonel Shaw removed his cigar from between his lips and said, "I will."[10] The men cheered loudly and were then ordered to lie down while waiting for the other troops to form on the battlefield. The Fifty-fourth had been given the fatal honor of leading the charge.

Captain Emilio described the scene, which he said the survivors of the battle would never forget. The heavy sea-fog gathered in the east as the sun set in the west. Distant thunder mingled with the roar of cannon. Silently, the soldiers gathered—line after line of men in blue as far as the eyes could see. And in the distance stood the battle-scarred fort, its flag waving defiantly.[11]

The men, Emilio wrote, were unusually quiet. This was the test. The officers wondered whether the men of the Fifty-fourth had learned the lessons they'd tried to teach them. If these men failed, then so did the experiment. The young colonel—in his light blue trousers, close-fitting officer's jacket, with a sash around his waist—calmly reviewed his regiment. He told them to prove themselves as men "and reminded them that the eyes of thousands would look upon the night's work."[12]

Finally, at about 7:45 P.M., the command "Forward" pierced the sultry, smoky air, and the Fifty-fourth advanced toward the fort, fired on by the enemy as they moved at quick time. When they were within 200 yards (183m) of the fort, it "became a mound of fire, from which poured a stream of shot and shell." The men in front dropped like felled trees, but those behind them quickened their pace to double time and, "with waving swords barely seen in the darkness, the men closed the gaps, and with set jaws, panting breath, and bowed heads, charged on."[13]

As the Fifty-fourth rushed into the cannon fire, the dark night was shattered by explosions and flashes that illuminated the scene of men who were down—either dead or wounded. The men who survived the fire closed in on the fort, separated from them by a ditch. Some waded through the knee-deep water and were able to climb the slope, while the cannon and riflemen fired on them.

Sergeant William H. Carney of Company C carried the flag of the Fifty-fourth and placed it on the parapet of the fort. Colonel Shaw climbed the rampart and, standing there with sword raised, shouted, " 'Forward, Fifty-Fourth!' and then fell dead, shot through the heart. . . ."[14] The regiment, following orders, had not yet fired a shot.

Once they reached the parapet they fought hand to hand, but the regiment had been decimated. There were too few left to successfully take the fort, and the supporting Union soldiers were too slow in coming. "The charge of the Fifty-fourth had been made and repulsed before the arrival of any other troops."[15]

The men who survived the battle were either lying in the ditch or hanging onto the sides of the fort. It was as dangerous to retreat as it was to go forward, for there was fire in front of and behind the Fifty-fourth now that the supporting regiments were also firing on the fort.

Sergeant George E. Stephens of Company B described the scene to Captain Emilio: "Just at the very hottest moment of the struggle, a battalion or regiment charged up to the moat, halted, and did not attempt to cross it and join us, but from their position commenced to fire upon us. I was one of the men who shouted from where I stood, 'Don't fire on us. We are the Fifty-fourth.' I have heard it was a Maine Regiment."[16]

Sergeant Carney, suffering two serious wounds, was able to bring the flag off the parapet. Captain Emilio, with the help of two other officers, searched for survivors and took them to the rear. At midnight all was quiet. The neck of Morris Island had become a graveyard. The other regiments who charged the fort met the same fate as the Fifty-fourth. The Union lost 1,515 men, including 111 officers.

As the Massachusetts Fifty-fourth charges Fort Wagner,
their colonel, Robert Gould Shaw, is fatally wounded.

Frank Myers of Company K, who had an arm shattered in the battle, and Thomas Burgess of Company I were with Colonel Shaw when he died, and heard his last words. The colonel had the witnesses he wanted. The men of the Fifty-fourth had proven themselves. Every report on the battle spoke of their bravery. General Strong said, "The Fifty-fourth did well and nobly." Even a Confederate officer said, "Numbers of both black and white were killed on top of our breastworks as well as inside. The [Negroes] fought gallantly and [were] headed by as brave a colonel as ever lived."[17]

Charlotte Forten expressed her feelings about the events at Fort Wagner in her diary: "To-night comes news oh, so sad, so heart sickening. It is too terrible, too terrible to write. We can only hope it may not all be true. That our noble, beautiful young Colonel is killed, and the regt. cut to pieces! I cannot, cannot believe it. And yet I know it may be so. But oh, I am stunned, sick at heart. I can scarcely write." A few days later, on July 22, she wrote sadly about her voluntary work at the regimental hospital: "My hospital life began to-day . . . Mrs. Saxton gave me some sewing to do—mending the pantaloons and jackets of the poor fellows. (They are all of the 54th.) It was with a full heart that I sewed up bullet holes and bayonet cuts."[18]

The Confederates buried the colonel with his men in a common grave. Shaw's fellow officers were outraged, because there had been an opportunity, when the battle ended, for the Confederates to give the colonel's body to the Union troops for a proper officer's burial. His father, Francis George Shaw, declined to have his son's grave located once the Union gained control of the island. He wrote to General Gilmore, then commander of the Department of the South, on August 24, 1863, "I am informed that ef-

119

forts are to be made to recover the body of my son, Colonel Shaw of the Fifty-fourth Massachusetts Regiment which was buried at Fort Wagner. My object in writing is to say that such efforts are not authorized by me or any of my family, and that they are not approved by us. We hold that a soldier's most appropriate burial-place is on the field where he has fallen. . . ."[19]

The regiment's work did not end with the storming of Fort Wagner. They performed guard duty on the island and helped to erect the batteries that would be used in the final siege of Fort Wagner. They did hard fatigue duty at the front and were not allowed time for drill or training. Fort Wagner was bombed for the next fifty-eight days. Finally, on September 7, 1863, Fort Sumter was taken and Fort Wagner evacuated. Susie King Taylor described the gruesome aftermath of the battle and the siege of Charleston:

> Fort Wagner being only a mile [1.6 km] from our camp, I went there two or three times a week, and would go up on the ramparts to watch the gunners send their shells into Charleston (which they did every fifteen minutes) and had a full view of the city from that point. Outside of the fort were many skulls lying about; I have often moved them to one side out of the path. . . . I had become accustomed to worse things and did not feel as I might have earlier in my camp life.[20]

The Fifty-fourth went to Florida in February 1864, and then returned to South Carolina in April, when they saw action again, performed more grueling fatigue duty on James Island, participated in the siege of Charleston, and guarded a prison camp housing 560 Confederate officers. They fought at Honey Hill, South Carolina, as part of the Coastal Division made up of other USCT and white troops.

Sergeant William H. Carney of the Massachusetts
Fifty-fourth Regiment was awarded the
Congressional Medal of Honor for his
bravery in the Battle of Fort Wagner.

On February 27, 1865, the Fifty-fourth entered Charleston, burned and destroyed by the war. The black residents gave the regiment a joyful welcome as it marched victoriously up Meeting and King streets. Most of the white inhabitants had abandoned the city.

The regiment left Charleston and went to Georgetown, South Carolina, to engage in their last battle, on April 18, 1865, at Boykin's Mills.

On September 2, 1865, at 9 A.M., the regiment arrived at Boston, where they were mustered out of the service. Vogelsang and Swails returned as lieutenants—a monumental achievement in the face of the military's opposition to black officers. William Carney was remembered for his bravery at Fort Wagner and received a Congressional Medal of Honor. Young Sufshay the drummer boy, Colonel Shaw, and five hundred other men and officers, however, did not return to the city they had left two years earlier.

The regiment had sailed from Boston in 1863 with an enrollment of 1,354 officers and enlisted men, and returned with 854 men and officers. The regiment had performed every kind of military duty asked of it, from building bridges to charging into artillery fire and facing certain death.

They had passed the test.

XII

FIGHTING MEN

Brethren, arise, arise! Strike for your lives and liberties. Now is the day and the hour . . . the days of slavery are numbered.

HENRY HIGHLAND GARNET

On the morning of February 20, 1864, the sound of marching feet could be heard through the woods. Some of the soldiers sang a marching song, "We're bound for Tallahassee in the morning." Actually the three black regiments and six white regiments—including smaller units of artillery and cavalry—were headed toward Olustee, an area fifty miles (80 km) west of Jacksonville, Florida.

"From a clear sky the warm sun glistened and gleamed through the tall pines bordering the pathway. About every hour the brigade halted for a short rest."[1]

Some of the white troops led the march and shots rang out when they met a few Confederate cavalry at an old mill. At about 1:30 in the afternoon, brief fighting broke out, until the skirmishers were stopped at a point where a railroad and a wagon road met and crossed. This crossroads where the opposing forces met would be the battlefield known as Olustee. The white regiments began to line up and went into the battle first. They took a sound beating from the Confederates, who had more troops. The men of the Seventh New Hampshire scattered in confusion but re-formed. The black brigade (three black regiments) was sent into the slaughter next.

The Eighth United States Colored Troops, "which had never been in battle . . . came up and filed to the right, when they were met with a most terrific shower of musketry and shell."[2] One of the officers said, "They had reported to me only two or three days before; I was afterward told that they had never had a day's practice in loading and firing. Old troops, finding themselves so greatly over-matched, would have run a little and re-formed—with or without orders."[3] The regiment started out with 550 men and lost 30, including their colonel.

At about 2:30 P.M. the Fifty-fourth and another regiment—the remainder of the black brigade— were ordered into the fight. Yelling "Three cheers for Massachusetts and seven dollars a month!" they rapidly discarded their blankets, haversacks, and knapsacks, as they moved at the double quick. When they reached the battleground they saw the wounded and dead. The white regiments were coming off the field. "We're badly whipped. You'll all get killed," the retreating troops told the new arrivals.[4] Stephen Swails, now an acting sergeant major in the Fifty-fourth, received a head wound in that action. The Fifty-fourth, however, did not suffer as many losses as the other regiments even though it remained on the field after they had retreated. A newspaper reporter wrote that "The two colored regiments had stood in the gap and saved the army."[5]

Again, the USCT were getting a chance to perform as soldiers. They had shown their mettle at Port

Hudson, and Milliken's Bend, and at Fort Wagner in 1863. They'd proven that they could stand and fight as well as white soldiers.

General David Hunter had seen as far back as 1862 the practicality and necessity of using black soldiers in the war effort. There were not enough white troops to hold the captured Sea Islands, and had it not been for the crucial role played by the USCT in 1863 and 1864, there is a good possibility that the islands would have been recaptured by the Confederates, and that Fort Sumter would have been reoccupied.

In the years 1864 and 1865, the black regiments saw the most action. Though they still performed a great deal of fatigue duty and made up 65 percent of the 27,876 Union soldiers that garrisoned forts from Kentucky to New Orleans, they fought on the frontier in Tennessee. Black regiments participated in the final assault on Mobile, Alabama, in 1865 and black regiments played an important role in the army's final assault on the South.[6]

Colonel Higginson wrote that Union General William T. Sherman's "march to the sea" through Georgia signaled the end of the Confederacy. When General Sherman reached Port Royal, South Carolina, he found that it was mainly the USCT that held the territory. "Next to the merit of those who made the march was that of those who held open the door. That service will always remain among the laurels of the black regiments."[7]

As part of the effort to aid General Sherman's march the Coast Division was organized. The division consisted of about 5,000 men and included seven USCT regiments. Part of the division had a major encounter with the rebels at Honey Hill, South Carolina, in the district of Beaufort.

On November 30, 1864, 1,400 Confederate troops

125

Black regiments played an important role
in the battles in 1864 and 1865.

waited behind a semicircular line of earthworks that ended at a pine forest on the right, with a swamp before the earthworks and a shallow creek running through the swamp. At 8:30 A.M., as the advance Union troops composed of white and black units reached Honey Hill, Confederate cannons opened fire. The Thirty-second USCT attempted to advance and cross the creek.

The Southerners held a good position behind their earthworks with the bushes and shrubs of the swamp for cover. General Edward Potter, leading the first brigade of advancing skirmishers, put his troops into the fight. The black regiments followed. All of the Union troops faced terrible artillery fire from the Confederate cannons. The Fifty-fifth Massachusetts lost "over one hundred men in five minutes."[8]

The Twenty-fifth Ohio and the Thirty-second USCT forced the Confederates on their left back to their defenses, but at a great sacrifice, losing many men in that long battle. The Union forces could not take Honey Hill and were forced, in the end, to retreat. The Fifty-fifth covered the Union retreat, occupying the same position that the Fifty-fourth had held at Olustee. Colonel Fox of the Fifty-fifth Massachusetts wrote in his diary:

> The patience, cheerfulness, and good conduct of the regiment during this month's campaign, deserve especial mention. Though there was much suffering from inclement weather, from scanty clothing, and often from short rations, few complaints were heard. Hard work was not grumbled at; and, recognized in their rights as soldiers, the men willingly accepted the hardships of the field, while striving to crush the rebellion and elevate their race. Especially to be noticed were the courage, patience, and cheerfulness of the wounded through the long, rough march following the battle of Honey Hill.[9]

A Confederate paper, the *Savannah Republican*, reported that "The Negroes, as usual, formed the advance and had nearly reached the creek, when our batteries opened upon them down the road. . . . This threw them into temporary confusion; but the entire force, estimated at five thousand, was quickly restored to order, and thrown into a line of battle parallel with our own, up and down the margin of the swamp. Thus the battle raged from eleven in the morning till dark."[10] The article suggests, as the Southerners had charged previously, that black soldiers were being misused by the Union. It does seem clear that in some of the actions—Fort Wagner, Port Hudson, Honey Hill, and later battles in Virginia— poor judgment and planning on the part of Union commanders led to unnecessary losses.

One of the captains in the Fifty-fifth Regiment said in the Philadelphia *Weekly Times*, "The generalship displayed was not equal to the soldierly qualities of the troops engaged." The commanders had made poor preparations for the battle and, once again, the Southerners were able to use the natural terrain to offset the Union's advantage of larger forces.[11]

The black and the white regiments that comprised the Coast Division garrisoned the coastal areas of South Carolina, Georgia, and Florida; performed fatigue duty, and also continued to fight. While these final operations of the war were continuing on the southern coast, the giant armies of both sides were preparing to clash in Virginia, and the public's attention turned in that direction.

XIII

FINAL BATTLES

I was attracted by the remarks of a white soldier as we left the fort. He looked at the colored troops and said, "Well, they are taking those colored men to their slaughter pen in front of Petersburg."

ISAAC J. HILL,
Twenty-ninth Regiment of Connecticut Colored Troops

The USCT in General Burnside's corps had been drilling and training for several weeks. Their officers took the men through exercise after exercise on charging fortifications. The soldiers drilled rigorously, for they were proud and excited to be part of the thirty-eight black regiments in the Army of the James and the Army of the Potomac. The black regiments had been chosen to lead the assault in a novel plan to capture Petersburg, Virginia, in the summer of 1864. Milton Holland's regiment, the Fifth USCT, was among the thirty-eight.

On June 24, 1864, the army began digging a tunnel, that led to the Confederate earthworks in Petersburg. The tunnel would be mined with explosives to blast away the fort that barred Union advancement into Petersburg. From there, Union troops would march right into Richmond, the Confederate capital.

The plan was that once the explosives were detonated, the USCT troops would lead the charge through the opening—the crater—created by the blast. They would attack to the right and the left of the fort, thus widening the breach. The rest of the corps would follow and take another fort to the rear. Holland had been waiting for such an opportunity ever since 1861, when he left school and tried to join the army. This would be his time to earn his glory.

On July 30, 1864, after the preparations were made to set off the explosion, Holland's regiment, along with all of the other USCT units, waited for the signal to charge. They were to fire their guns into the enemy's lines, then jump over the low wall in front of the fort and charge through the crater.

While the men waited for their signal, they received disappointing news. A white division was to be substituted for the black regiments. Holland would have to wait for his day of glory. Captain Rickard, a USCT regimental officer, said, "Had the plan been followed, no doubt the war would have ended on that day."[1]

The plan was not followed. General George Meade, who was in command of the operation, decided that he did not want black troops to lead the attack, for if they were unsuccessful the army would be accused of using black soldiers as cannon fodder in such an experimental operation. General Grant agreed with Meade. Grant said, "General Burnside wanted to put his colored division in front, and I believe if he had done so it would have been a success. . . . I agreed with General Meade in his objection to that plan . . . if it should prove a failure, it would then be said, and very properly, that we were shoving those people ahead to get killed because we did not care anything about them."[2]

Captain Rickard wrote of his regiment's disappointment:

> We had expected we were to lead the assault, and had been for several weeks drilling our men with this idea in view. Both our officers and men were much disappointed, as it was an opportunity to show what they could do, and there was not an officer but would have staked everything that we would break through their lines .... When all preparations were made, we lay down for a little sleep, and were awakened shortly after daylight by the explosion and the terrible discharge of cannon, that made the ground tremble as by an earthquake.[3]

The attempt ended in a terrible slaughter. The white divisions who led the assault after the explosion were battle weary and ill prepared. Once the tunnel had been mined and they entered the crater—which was 170 feet (51.8m) long and 60 to 80 feet (18 to 21m) wide—they became a confused mass of fifteen thousand men not knowing where to turn in the maze of Confederate pits and trenches.

The Southerners recovered from the initial shock of the explosion and swept the crater with deadly fire. The Union soldiers, although thirty feet (9m) into Southern lines and sheltered from the Confederate cannons, failed to charge the fort.

The black soldiers were ordered in after about an hour. What they saw must have looked like a scene from hell. Thousands of soldiers were milling about in confusion. Helpless wounded and dying men blocked passages, and other soldiers were trying to retreat to the rear, away from the artillery fire. Hindered by the retreating white forces, the black soldiers surged ahead as best they could. "The black troops advance . . . followed by not one white soldier and are cut to pieces at the other end."[4]

The Union troops, at the left, meet the
Confederates at the Battle of the Crater.

Captain Rickard described what happened:

Finally, about 7:30 A.M. we got the order for the colored division to charge. My brigade followed Siegfried's at the double quick. Arrived at the "crater" a part of the first brigade entered; the "crater" was already too full, that I could easily see.

I swung my column to the right. The pits were different from any in our own lines . . . a labyrinth of bombproofs and magazines, with passages between. My brigade moved gallantly on right over the bombproofs and over the men of the first division. As we mounted the pits, a deadly enfilade [line of gunfire] from eight guns on our right and a deadly cross-fire decimated us. . . . at this time hundreds of heroes "carved in ebony" fell. These black men commanded the admiration of every beholder on that day.

Sergeant Decatur Dorsey of the Thirty-ninth Infantry USCT won a Congressional Medal of Honor for his bravery at this battle. Advancing before his regiment, he placed the national flag on the Confederate fort. When his regiment was forced to retreat, he carried the flag back and encouraged the men to keep fighting.

There are several reasons for the failure of the Battle of the Crater. The divisions that led the assault were unprepared. They were battle fatigued from the Petersburg campaign that had been in operation since June. It seems also that a mixture of debilitating racism and fear of being executed by the Confederates if captured with black soldiers kept the white troops from following the black soldiers once they (USCT) had managed to penetrate about two hundred more yards (183m) into enemy lines.

George L. Kilmer, an officer of the Fourteenth New York Heavy Artillery, went into the crater with the first wave and reported afterward that when the USCT moved forward to charge the fort, some of the white soldiers refused to follow them. Pandemonium broke out when the black soldiers could not continue the assault and started to retreat and come back into the crater. "Some colored men came into the crater, and there they found a worse fate than death in the charge. . . . It has been positively asserted, that white men bayoneted blacks who fell back into the crater."[5]

The black troops were not given an opportunity to demonstrate their skill as soldiers at Petersburg. General Benjamin Butler felt that the army was not sincerely committed to using black soldiers in major military operations.

On September 29, 1864, however, the general decided to include a black brigade as part of the force participating in the action at New Market Heights, also called Chaffin's Farm, Virginia. The goal was to take a fortification that they had failed to capture previously. Sergeant Milton Holland's regiment was part of the brigade that stormed Chaffin's Farm. Sergeant major Christian A. Fleetwood's regiment was there also.

In the early dawn of September 29, 1864, the men of the USCT, with bayonets drawn and the caps removed from their guns, stormed the battlements at Chaffin's Farm. The fighting was fierce as musket shells rained down on the front ranks of the black soldiers. Holland, now a sergeant major, saw that all the officers of his company were either killed or wounded. He was also wounded, but he remained on the battlefield and commanded his company. The black brigade was able to capture an important Confederate position.

Generals Grant and Butler rode over to the battlefield to review the troops. Butler was so impressed with Holland's leadership abilities and bravery that he made him a captain on the spot. Sergeant-Major Holland had achieved his moment of glory. General Butler awarded him a medal and he also later, received a Congressional Medal of Honor from President Lincoln.

The War Department, however, would not approve Holland's promotion to captain because he was of African descent. Holland remained a sergeant-major, the highest rank a black soldier was allowed to attain. The Ohio schoolboy distinguished himself even though he didn't get the promotion he rightly deserved.

Eleven other black soldiers—including Sergeant Major Christian A. Fleetwood—received the Congressional Medal of Honor for their bravery at Chaffin's Farm.

At the same time that the black regiments were fighting at Chaffin's Farm, other USCT units were storming nearby Fort Gilmer. J. M. Califf, a lieutenant in the Seventh Regiment of United States Colored Troops, described the attack on Fort Gilmer in his history of the regiment. When Captain Weiss was given the order to charge the fort, he looked at his men and said that he could not take a fort with so few men. Shaking his head, he muttered, "I will try, but it can't be done."

Sadly he ordered his men to charge. The orderly blue lines of black troops moved forward in quick time, and the sounds of their feet tramping in unison sounded through the early-morning air.

"Double quick," Captain Weiss shouted and the lines of troops, as if one body, raced toward the fort. Not a man hesitated or faltered; their lines were as orderly as if they were practicing drill.

The men did not stop running, even when they reached the ditch in front of the fort. Every man jumped into the ditch, which quickly became a death trap as the fort's defenders hammered them with shell after shell. The soldiers gathered around one wall that was out of range of the artillery fire.

Captain Weiss assessed the situation and then gave the order to climb the parapet. The soldiers began to scramble up toward the fort, raising one another over the wall. Thirty to forty men were lifted over, but as they tried to enter the fort, they were forced back with hand grenades and shells.

Wounded and dead men fell back into the ditch. Weiss repeated his order and again the men lifted one another over the wall. Now they were bombarded with grape shot and shells. Weiss ordered a third try. The Confederates shouted, "Surrender! Surrender!" One black soldier, Perry Wallace, fired into the fort as he was lifted over the wall. "We will show you how to surrender," he yelled, before tumbling back into the ditch. He was hit by artillery fire.

Captain Weiss and his storming party were all killed. Only one man from Weiss's company survived the battle—George W. Washington, of Company D. Other troops followed this initial attempt to take the fort, but had to surrender as the Confederates showered them with artillery fire.

The first four companies that stormed the fort were completely annihilated. "In the end, although black units comprised only a small portion of the Federal force in the battle, they suffered 43 percent of the losses."[6]

This was a sad day for the Seventh Regiment USCT. Many of the soldiers knew they were being watched by a mostly unsympathetic public. They knew they were fighting not just the Confederate army; they were also fighting stereotypes and negative images. They did not capture Fort Gilmer, but no one could say that they did not perform bravely in the face of certain death.

Even the Confederates took notice of the bravery of the USCT. One of their newspapers printed a letter suggesting that the black men still held in slavery in the South should be armed. "Fort Gilmer proved the other day that they [blacks] would fight. They raised each other on the parapet to be shot as they appeared above."

USCT soldiers were kept busy for the rest of the year. Milton Holland and the other USCT men who had survived the Battle of the Crater, Chaffin's Farm, and Fort Gilmer faced the Confederates in fighting at Fair Oaks and Darbytown Road, Virginia, on October 27 and 28. They were involved too in a campaign against Fort Fisher in North Carolina. They also performed garrison duty and the never-ending, grueling fatigue duty.

On December 3, 1864, for the first time in American military history, an entire army corps was composed of black troops. The War Department organized the XXV Corps, with men drawn primarily from USCT units of the Department of Virginia and North Carolina under Major General Godfrey Weitzel. From May 1864 to April 1865, the Union armies battered the Confederates.

The war was finally coming to an end in the spring of 1865. USCT soldiers marched into Wilmington, North Carolina, in March of that year. In the same month the Fifty-first United States Colored Infantry marched into a fallen Montgomery, Alabama, to the cheers of the city's freed black population. Private Hill, of the Twenty-ninth Regiment of Connecticut Colored Troops, described the activity before the fall of Richmond and General Lee's surrender at Appomatox:

At 10 A.M. on the 29th inst. [February] we moved from the breast-works on the left of Fort Harrison to the hill in the centre, where we built a tower overlooking the rebel works into Richmond. We remained there four weeks, and on the 27th of March we moved again. Part of the 29th rested in Fort Harrison and the 2d Brigade in . . . General Birney's Headquarters. All was quiet here until the 1st of April when all was in readiness, and the order was given to strike tents and move into Richmond.[7]

There was some justice in the fact that the USCT were among the first to march into the fallen Confederate capital. On April 4, 1865, President Abraham Lincoln visited Richmond, Virginia, which had been abandoned by the Confederates. Hill described the president's entry into the city:

I was standing on the bank of the James River viewing the scene of desolation when a boat, pulled by twelve sailors, came up the stream. It contained President Lincoln and his son. . . . In some way the colored people on the bank of the river ascertained that the tall man wearing the black hat was President Lincoln. There was a sudden shout and clapping of hands. . . . I have never witnessed such rejoicing in all my life. As the President passed along the street the colored people waved their handkerchiefs, hats and bonnets. . . .[8]

On April 9, 1865, Lee surrendered at Appomatox and one of the most devasting wars the United States had ever experienced ended. Approximately 180,000 men of African descent, 10 percent of the Union army, had helped the federal government save the Union, and end legal slavery in the United States. The USCT participated in 449 military engagements, 39 of which were major battles[9]

The black soldiers had fought against two enemies. As part of the Union army they fought and worked along with their white counterparts to win a

With the war and slavery at an end,
the black population of Richmond, Virginia,
cheers President Lincoln, April 3, 1865.

war. Their most difficult battles, however, were often the ones waged against the entrenched racial attitudes held by those who absolutely refused to recognize the humanity of people of African descent. Racism limited the role that blacks could play as soldiers—some regiments saw only fatigue and garrison duty. Those regiments that were allowed to fight went into battle burdened with the knowledge that the slightest failure on their part would be magnified and used to demonstrate black inferiority by those in the army, the government, or the press whose views were shaped by anti-black sentiments.

The black soldiers served even though they would not be afforded the rights of prisoners of war if caught by the enemy, did not receive equal pay, and had little opportunity to become officers. They faced the fires of war and hatred hoping that people of African descent in America would finally have the right to "life, liberty and the pursuit of happiness."

The experiment was a success.

EPILOGUE

"Will the Negro fight?" As a problem, it has been solved, as a question it has been answered, and as a fact it is as established as the eternal hills.

CHRISTIAN A. FLEETWOOD,
former sergeant major,
Fourth United States Colored Troops

War is the greatest of human tragedies. As in all tragedies, there are unknown people who attempt to ease the pain of the sufferers. Charlotte Forten and Susie King Taylor left written records of their Civil War service. And, fortunately, the life and deeds of brave Harriet Tubman were not forgottn, either.

There were, however, other Charlottes and Harriets and Susies whose actions were not recorded, or singled out and remembered, but who also taught in the army camps, did the laundry, mended jackets torn by bullets and bayonets, and tried to heal and comfort soldiers ripped apart by cannon and gunfire.

Like Harriet Tubman, there were other women and men who freed themselves and helped others escape to freedom, too. Many gave invaluable service to the army and the navy as scouts and spies—returning again and again to Confederate territory to bring out other fugitives and to get information about Confederate troop movements and plans. The navy accepted enlistment from fugitives as early as 1861, and many of them provided useful intelligence. One, James Lawson, became known as the hero of the Potomac after repeated trips back and forth across the river to gather information for the navy about Confederate activities in Virginia.

Many black people who did not escape the Confederacy and remained in the South helped the federal government also. Black men and women sheltered and protected Union soldiers—white as well as black—who escaped from Confederate prison camps. In some cases they helped the soldiers to escape. The black Southern population also helped Union soldiers caught behind Confederate lines after a battle to find their way back to their military units. Many white Union soldiers changed their racist attitudes after they were aided by black Southerners.

And the black inhabitants were there to give rousing welcomes to the USCT when they entered Montgomery, Alabama; Charleston, South Carolina; Richmond, Virginia; and other Southern cities at the end of the war.

The names of these people are unknown, shrouded in the past—the soldiers, the officers who fought and died with them, and the civilian men and women, freeborn and captive slave, who supported the Union, the USCT and, most of all, the ideals of freedom and justice.

The Thirteenth Amendment, abolishing slavery in the United States, was ratified by Congress in 1865; however, the issue of equality was still not settled. Black Civil War veterans wanted to be recog-

A woodcut from the period presents
a scene of black troops liberating
slaves in Charleston, South Carolina.

nized as citizens protected by the Constitution, with
the right to vote.

The Fourteenth Amendment, ratified in 1868,
guaranteed citizenship to "all persons born or natu-
ralized in the United States." The Fifteenth Amendment, ratified in 1870, gave the vote to all male
citizens of the United States, "regardless of race,
color or previous condition of servitude." However, it
would be still another century before these rights
were fully realized by all American citizens of color.
As late as 1888 Frederick Douglass lamented: "We
see colored citizens shot down and driven from the
ballot box, and forget the services rendered by the
colored troops in the late war for the Union."

Ratification of the Thirteenth, Fourteenth, and
Fifteenth amendments to the Constitution was the
culmination of a long struggle waged by blacks and

those whites who believed that all people are created equal. These amendments brought America closer to its ideals of freedom and democracy, and ensured that the rights of citizenship would be available to future Americans who would come to these shores seeking freedom. Those rights and some of that freedom were gained through the sacrifices of the unsung heroes of the United States Colored Troops.

Once the Civil War ended most soldiers—black and white—wanted to return to civilian life. After a year of reconstruction duty (rebuilding the South after the war), the army was reduced. The United States did not maintain a large peacetime army. Only six black regiments were retained by the army after the war, but they marked the beginning of a slowly increasing acceptance of African Americans into the military.

The military service continued, however, to segregate black soldiers and white soldiers in separate units, with opportunities for blacks to become commissioned officers very limited. Benjamin O. Davis, the first black general, served as a colonel for ten years before he rose in rank during World War II. President Harry Truman encouraged integration of the armed forces near the end of World War II. However, it was not until 1951, during the Korean War, that the integration of black troops and white troops was accomplished.

NOTES

ONE
SAVE THE UNION

1. James M. McPherson, *The Negro's Civil War* (New York: Pantheon Books, 1965), 19.
2. McPherson, 21.
3. Peter Clark, *The Black Brigade of Cincinnati* (Cincinnati: Joseph B. Boyd, Printers, 1864), 4–5.
4. McPherson, 162.
5. Stefan Lorant, *Lincoln—A Picture Story of His Life* (New York: W. W. Norton & Company, Inc., 1969), 79.
6. John Hope Franklin and Franklin Moss, *From Slavery to Freedom*, 6th ed. (New York: Alfred A. Knopf, 1988), 73.
7. Franklin, 140–141.

TWO
FIGHTING FOR A CHANCE TO FIGHT

1. James M. McPherson, *The Negro's Civil War* (New York: Pantheon Books, 1965), 35.

2. Emma E. Edmonds, *Nurse and Spy in the Union Army* (Hartford: W. S. Williams & Co., 1865), 71.
    3. Thomas Wentworth Higginson, *Army Life In A Black Regi-
ment* (Boston: Fields, Osgood & Co., 1870; Reprint, New York:
Time-Life Books, Inc., 1982), 246.
    4. McPherson, 39.
    5. McPherson, 38.
    6. John S. Bowman, ed., *The Civil War Almanac* (New York:
World Almanac Publications, 1983), 110.

THREE
WORKING FOR THE REBELS

    1. Charles Wesle, "Negroes in the Confederate Army," *Journal of Negro History*, Vol. 4, #3 (1919), 244.
    2. James M. McPherson, *The Negro's Civil War* (New York: Pantheon Books, 1965), 24.
    3. Wesle, 242–43.
    4. Wesle, 244.
    5. Wesle, 244–45.
    6. McPherson, 25.
    7. McPherson, 26.
    8. McPherson, 24.
    9. Wesle, 246.
    10. Wesle, 247.
    11. Wesle, 249–50.
    12. Wesle, 251.

FOUR
HUNTER'S REGIMENT

    1. Much of the information for this chapter was drawn from Dudley T. Cornish, *The Sable Arm* (New York: Longmans Green & Co., 1956).
    2. Cornish, 34.
    3. Cornish, 35.
    4. The First Confiscation Act, signed August 6, 1861, allowed for Union seizure of all property used by the Confederates in the war. This property included black men held in slavery, who were used as laborers by the Confederate army.
    5. Cornish, 35.

6. Cornish, 37.
7. Cornish, 54.
8. Cornish, 38–49.
9. Christian A. Fleetwood, *The Negro As A Soldier* (Washington, D.C., Howard University Printer, 1895), 6.
10. Cornish, 46.

FIVE
WHO WILL LEAD?

1. David W. Blight, *Frederick Douglass' Civil War* (Baton Rouge: Louisiana State University Press, 1989), 106.
2. William H. Chenery, *The Fourteenth Regiment Rhode Island Heavy Artillery (Colored)* (Providence: Snow & Farnham Printers, 1898), 17.
3. Joseph T. Glatthaar, *Forged in Battle* (New York: The Free Press, 1990), 10.
4. Charlotte Forten Grimké, *The Journals of Charlotte Forten Grimké*, Brenda Stevenson, ed. (New York: Oxford University Press, 1988), 405 and 490. Charlotte Forten Grimké was a member of a wealthy and prominent free black Philadelphia family.
5. Glatthaar, 37.
6. Glatthaar, 39.
7. Glatthaar, 55.
8. Glatthaar, 89.

SIX
CALL TO ARMS

1. Charles S. Wainwright, *The Personal Journals of Charles S. Wainwright,* Allan Nevins, ed. (New York: Harcourt, Brace and World, 1962), 155.
2. Luis F. Emilio, *A Brave Black Regiment: History of the Fifty-Fourth Regiment of Massachusetts Volunteer Infantry* (Boston: Boston Book Company, 1894; Reprint, Salem: Ayer Company Publishers, Inc., 1990) 2–3.
3. Emilio, 9.
4. William H. Chenery, *The Fourteenth Regiment Rhode Island Heavy Artillery (Colored)* (Providence: Snow & Farnham Printers, 1898), 5.

5. Chenery, 6.

6. Frank H. Taylor, *Philadelphia in the Civil War 1861–65,* (Published by the City, 1913), 188.

7. James M. McPherson, *The Negro's Civil War* (New York: Pantheon Books, 1965), 71.

8. Report of the New York Association for Colored Volunteers (1863), 20.

9. New York Association for Colored Volunteers, 14.

10. David W. Blight, *Frederick Douglass' Civil War,* (Baton Rouge: Louisiana State University Press, 1989), 159.

11. Joseph J. Califf, *Record of the Services of the Seventh Regiment* (Providence: E. L. Freeman & Co., Printers, 1878), 11.

12. Califf, 12.

13. James T. Ayers, *The Civil War Diary of James T. Ayers,* John Hope Franklin, ed. (Springfield: Occasional Publications of the Illinois State Historical Society, 1947), 43.

14. Dudley T. Cornish, *The Sable Arm* (New York: Longmans, Green & Co., 1956), 257.

SEVEN
THE MEN

1. Thomas Wentworth Higginson, *Army Life In A Black Regiment,* (Boston: Fields, Osgood, & Co., 1870; Reprint, New York: Time-Life Books, Inc., 1982), 5.

2. Dudley T. Cornish, *The Sable Arm* (New York: Longmans, Green & Co., 1956), 256.

3. Cornish, 256.

4. William Wells Brown, *The Negro in the American Rebellion* (New York: Lee & Shepard, 1867; Reprint, New York: Citadel Press, 1971), 263.

5. Joseph T. Glatthaar, *Forged in Battle* (New York: The Free Press, 1990), 124.

6. Glatthaar, 125.

7. Higginson, 57.

8. Higginson, 62–63.

9. Charlotte Forten Grimké, *The Journals of Charlotte Forten Grimké,* Brenda Stevenson, ed. (New York: Oxford University Press, 1988), 429–430.

10. William H. Chenery, *The Fourteenth Regiment Rhode Island Heavy Artillery (Colored)* (Providence: Snow & Farnham Printers, 1898), 10.

11. Edward M. Main, *The Story of the Third United States Colored Cavalry,* (Globe Printing Co., 1908; Reprint, New York: Negro Universities Press, 1970), 12.
12. Main, 58–59.
13. Thomas J. Morgan, *Colored Troops in the Army of the Cumberland* (Personal Narratives, Rhode Island Soldiers and Sailors Historical Society, 3rd series, no. 13, 1885), 11–14.
14. Glatthaar, 272.
15. Morgan, 14.

EIGHT
CAMP LIFE

1. Thomas Wentworth Higginson, *Army Life In A Black Regiment* (Boston: Fields, Osgood & Co., 1870; Reprint, Time-Life Books, Inc., 1982), 26.
2. Higginson, 18.
3. Luis F. Emilio, *A Brave Black Regiment: History of the Fifty-Fourth Regiment of Massachusetts Volunteer Infantry* (Boston: Boston Book Company, 1894; Reprint, Salem: Ayer Company Publishers, Inc., 1990), 125.
4. George R. Sherman, *The Negro as a Soldier* (Providence: Personal Narratives, Rhode Island Soldiers and Sailors Historical Society, series no. 7, 1913), 17–18.
5. Thomas J. Morgan, *Colored Troops in the Army of the Cumberland* (Personal Narratives, Rhode Island Soldiers and Sailors Historical Society, 3rd series, no. 13, 1885), 23–24.
6. Higginson, 25.
7. Gerda Lerner, ed. *Black Women in White America* (New York: Vintage Books, 1973), 100–101.
8. J. M. Addeman, "Reminiscences of Two years With the Colored Troops," (Personal Narratives, Rhode Island Soldiers and Sailors Historical Society, series 2, no. 7, 1880), 26–27.
9. Joseph T. Glatthaar, *Forged in Battle* (New York: The Free Press, 1990), 103.
10. Morgan, 18.
11. Higginson, 47.
12. Edward M. Main, *The Story of the Third United States Colored Cavalry* (Globe Printing Co., 1908; Reprint, New York: Negro Universities Press, 1970), 59.
13. Morgan, 13–14.
14. Glatthaar, 109.

NINE
THE OTHER ENEMY

1. Victor Hicken, *Illinois in the Civil War* (Urbana: University of Illinois Press, 1966), 133.
2. Charlotte Forten Grimké, *The Journals of Charlotte Forten Grimké*, Brenda Stevenson, ed. (New York: Oxford University Press, 1988), 389.
3. Benjamin F. McIntyre, *Federals on the Frontier: The Diary of Benjamin F. McIntyre—1862–1864*, 326–327.
4. Theodore F. Upson, *With Sherman to the Sea* Bloomington: Indiana University Press, 1958), 149.
5. Thomas Wentworth Higginson, *Army Life In A Black Regiment* (Boston: Fields, Osgood, & Co., 1870; Reprint, New York: Time-Life Books, Inc., 1982), 3.
6. Thomas J. Morgan, *Colored Troops in the Army of the Cumberland* (Personal Narratives, Rhode Island Soldiers and Sailors Historical Society, 3rd series, no. 13, 1885), 18–19.
7. Luis F. Emilio, *A Brave Black Regiment: History of the Fifty-Fourth Regiment of Massachusetts Volunteer Infantry* (Boston: Boston Book Company, 1894; Reprint, Salem: Ayer Company Publishers, Inc., 1990), 125.
8. Morgan, 20.
9. Emilio, 217.
10. Higginson, 29.
11. Isaac J. Hill, *A Sketch of the 29th Regiment of Connecticut Colored Troops*, (Baltimore: Daugherty, Maguire, & Co., 1867), 11–12.
12. William Wells Brown, *The Negro in the American Rebellion* (New York: Lee & Shepard, 1867; Reprint, New York: Citadel Press, 1971), 98–99.
13. Joseph T. Glatthaar, *Forged in Battle* (New York: The Free Press, 1990), 115.
14. Glatthaar, 173
15. Susie King Taylor, *Reminiscences of My Life in Camp* (New York: Arno Press, 1968), 16.
16. Emilio, 221.
17. Higginson, 261.
18. Dudley T. Cornish, *The Sable Arm* (New York: Longmans, Green & Co., 1956), 214.
19. Brown, 20.
20. Glatthaar, 187–195.

21. Benjamin Quarles, *The Negro in the Civil War 1861–65* (Boston: Little, Brown and Company, 1953), 204.
22. Brown, 176.
23. Emilio, 429.

TEN
SOLDIER'S WORK

1. Many of the details in this chapter are from Joseph T. Glatthaar, *Forged in Battle* (New York: The Free Press, 1990).
2. William Wells Brown, *The Negro in the American Rebellion* (New York: Lee & Shepard, 1867; Reprint, New York: Citadel Press, 1971), 168.
3. Brown, 169.
4. Brown, 174.
5. Brown, 171.
6. Brown, 171.
7. Glatthaar, 129.
8. Glatthaar, 129.
9. Glatthaar, 133.
10. Glatthaar, 135.
11. Glatthaar, 135.

ELEVEN
CAN I GET A WITNESS?

1. Much of the information contained in this chapter is drawn from Luis F. Emilio, *A Brave Black Regiment: History of the Fifty-Fourth Regiment of Massachusetts Volunteer Infantry* (Boston: Boston Book Company, 1894; Reprint, Salem: Ayer Company Publishers, Inc., 1990.)
2. Emilio, 49.
3. Emilio, 57.
4. Emilio, 58.
5. Emilio, 61–62.
6. Emilio, 66.
7. Emilio, 70.
8. Emilio, 70.
9. Emilio, 72.
10. Emilio, 77.
11. Emilio, 76.

12. Emilio, 78.
13. Emilio, 80.
14. Emilio, 82.
15. Emilio, 84.
16. Emilio, 93.
17. Emilio, 95.
18. Charlotte Forten Grimké, *The Journals of Charlotte Forten Grimké*, Brenda Stevenson, ed. (New York: Oxford University Press, 1988), 494–495.
19. Emilio, 102–103.
20. Susie King Taylor, *Reminiscences of My Life in Camp* (New York: Arno Press, 1968), 31.

TWELVE
FIGHTING MEN

1. Luis F. Emilio, *A Brave Black Regiment: History of the Fifty-Fourth Regiment of Massachusetts Volunteer Infantry* (Boston: Boston Book Company, 1894; Reprint, Salem: Ayer Company Publishers, Inc., 1990), 159.
2. Williams Wells Brown, *The Negro in the American Rebellion* (New York: Lee & Shepard, 1867; Reprint, New York: Citadel Press, 1971), 218.
3. Dudley T. Cornish, *The Sable Arm* (New York: Longmans, Green & Co., 1956), 267.
4. Emilio, 163.
5. Emilio, 167.
6. Cornish, 266.
7. Thomas Wentworth Higginson, *Army Life In a Black Regiment* (Boston: Fields, Osgood & Co., 1870; Reprint, New York: Time-Life Books, Inc., 1982), 263.
8. Emilio, 243
9. Charles Bernard Fox, *Record of the Service of the Fifty-Fifth Massachusetts Volunteer Infantry* (Cambridge: John Wilson and Son Press, 1868), 47.
10. Brown, 261.
11. Emilio, 252.

THIRTEEN
FINAL BATTLES

1. James H. Rickard, *Services with Colored Troops in Burnside's*

Corps. (Personal Narratives, Rhode Island Soldiers and Sailors Historical Society, 1894), 25–26.

2. Dudley T. Cornish, *The Sable Arm* (New York: Longmans, Green & Co., 1956), 274.
3. Rickard, 26–27.
4. John S. Bowman, ed., *The Civil War Almanac* (New York: World Almanac Publications, 1983), 218.
5. Cornish, 276.
6. Joseph T. Glatthaar, *Forged in Battle* (New York: The Free Press, 1990), 151.
7. Isaac J. Hill, *A Sketch of the 29th Regiment of Connecticut Colored Troops* (Baltimore: Daugherty, Maguire & Co., 1867), 25.
8. Hill, 26.
9. Cornish, 265.

BIBLIOGRAPHY

Bennett, Lerone Jr. *Before the Mayflower*, 5th ed. Chicago: Johnson Publishing Company, Inc., 1982.

Blight, David W. *Frederick Douglass' Civil War*. Baton Rouge: Louisiana State University Press, 1989.

Brawley, Benjamin. *Early Negro American Writers*. New York: Books for Libraries Press, 1935.

The Civil War Almanac, John S. Bowman, ed. New York: World Almanac Publications, 1963.

Congressional Report, Fort Pillow Massacre, April, 1864.

Cornish, Dudley T. *The Sable Arm*. New York: Longmans, Green & Co., 1956.

Franklin, John Hope, and Alfred A. Moss, Jr. *From Slavery to Freedom*, 6th ed. New York: Alfred A. Knopf, 1988.

Glatthaar, Joseph T. *Forged in Battle*. New York: The Free Press, 1990.

Harding, Vincent. *There Is a River*. New York: Harcourt Brace Jovanovich, 1981.

Hicken, Victor. *Illinois in the Civil War*. Urbana: University of Illinois Press, 1966.

Lerner, Gerda, ed. *Black Women in White America*. New York: Vintage Books, 1973.

Lorant, Stefan. *Lincoln—A Picture Story of His Life*. New York: W. W. Norton & Company, Inc., 1969.

McPherson, James M. *Marching Toward Freedom*. New York: Alfred A. Knopf, 1965.

——*The Negro's Civil War*. New York: Pantheon Books, 1965.

Meltzer, Milton. *In Their Own Words*. New York: Thomas Y. Crowell, 1964.

Mitchell, Joseph B. "Negro Troops at Chaffin's Farms," *The Badge of Gallantry*. New York: The Macmillan Company, 1968.

Pleasants, Henry, Jr., and George H. Straley. *Inferno at Petersburg*. Radnor, Pa.: Chilton Company, 1961.

Quarles, Benjamin, *The Negero in the Civil War*. Boston: Little, Brown and Company, 1953.

Report of the New York Association for Colored Volunteers, 1863.

Taylor, Frank H. *Philadelphia in the Civil War 1861–65*. Published by the City, 1913.

Tyler, Mason Whiting. *Recollections of the Civil War*. New York: G. P. Putnam's Sons, 1912.

Upson, Theodore F. *With Sherman to the Sea*. Bloomington: Indiana University Press, 1958.

Wesle, Charles. "Negroes in the Confederate Army." *Journal of Negro History*, Vol. 4, #3 (1919): 239–53.

PRIMARY SOURCES

Addeman, J. M. "Reminiscences of Two Years With the Colored Troops," *Personal Narratives, Rhode Island Soldiers and Sailors Historical Society, series 2. no. 7*. 1880

Ayers, James T. *The Civil War Diary of James T. Ayers*. Springfield: Occasional Publications of the Illinois State Historical Society, 1947, John Hope Franklin, ed.

Brown, William Wells. *The Negro in the American Rebellion*. New York: Lee & Shepard, 1867. Reprint, New York: Citadel Press, 1971.

Califf, Joseph M. *Record of the Services of the Seventh Regiment*. Providence: E. L. Freeman & Co., Printers, 1878.

Chenery, William H. *The Fourteenth Regiment Rhode Island Heavy Artillery (Colored)*. Providence: Snow & Farnham Printers, 1898.

Clark, Peter. *The Black Brigade of Cincinnati*. Joseph B. Boyd, Printers.

Cowden, Robert. "A Brief Sketch of the Organization and Services of the Fifty-Ninth Regiment of United States Colored Infantry." Dayton: United Brethren Publishing House, 1883.

Dennett, George M. *History of the Ninth U.S.C. Troops.* Philadelphia: King and Baird Printers, 1866.

Edmonds, Emma E. *Nurse and Spy in the Union Army.* Hartford: W. S. Williams & Co., 1865.

Emilio, Luis F. *A Brave Black Regiment: History of the Fifty-Fourth Regiment of Massachusetts Volunteer Infantry.* Boston: Boston Book Company, 1894. Reprint, Salem: Ayer Company Publishers, Inc., 1990.

Fleetwood, Christian. *The Negro As A Soldier.* Washington, D.C.: Howard University Printer. 1895.

Fox, Charles Bernard. *Record of the Service of the Fifty-Fifth Massachusetts Volunteer Infantry.* Cambridge: John Wilson and Son Press, 1868.

Grimké, Charlotte Forten, *The Journals of Charlotte Forten Grimké*, Brenda Stevenson, ed. New York: Oxford University Press, 1988.

Higginson, Thomas Wentworth. *Army Life In A Black Regiment.* Boston: Fields, Osgood, & Co., 1870. Reprint, New York: Time-Life Books, Inc., 1982.

Hill, Isaac J. *A Sketch of the 29th Regiment of Connecticut Colored Troops.* Baltimore: Daugherty, Maguire & Co., 1867.

McIntyre, Benjamin F. *Federals on the Frontier: The Diary of Benjamin F. McIntyre—1862–1864.* Nannie M. Tilley, ed. Austin: University of Texas Press, [c. 1963].

Main, Edward M. *The Story of the Third United States Colored Cavalry.* Globe Printing Co., 1908. Reprint, New York: Negro Universities Press, 1970.

Morgan, Thomas J. *Colored Troops in the Army of the Cumberland.* Personal Narratives, Rhode Island Soldiers and Sailors Historical Society, 3rd series, no. 13. 1885.

Rickard, James H. *Services with Colored Troops in Burnsides Corps.* Personal Narratives, Rhode Island Soldiers and Sailors Historical Society, 1894.

Sherman, George R. *The Negro as a Soldier.* Providence: Personal Narratives, Rhode Island Soldiers and Sailors Historical Society, series no. 7, 1913.

Taylor, Susie King. *Reminiscences of My Life in Camp.* New York: Arno Press, 1968.

Wainwright, Charles S. *The Personal Journals of Charles S. Wainwright.* Allan Nevins, ed. New York: Harcourt Brace & World, 1962.

Yetman, Norman R. *Voices From Slavery.* New York: Holt, Rinehart and Winston, 1970.

Index